02233

Understanding Pupil Behaviour

D1739634

This book describes a system of successful classroom behaviour management techniques developed by the author over more than 25 years. It outlines the difficulties confronting teachers trying to manage pupils' misbehaviour in schools and describes four types of pupil who can be helped to behave responsibly.

In *Understanding Pupil Behaviour* Ramon (Rom) Lewis explains how pupils' behaviour can be categorised and how techniques can be introduced to deal with each category, however challenging the behaviour might be. The book goes on to provide a framework for long-term commitment by teachers to producing effective interactions with pupils.

Teachers, PGCE pupils and educational advisors looking for a handy guide to tried-and-tested behaviour management strategies, as well as those wanting a resource for delivering INSET training on the subject, will find all they need in this accessible book.

Ramon (Rom) Lewis is the author of *The Discipline Dilemma* and *Coping Scale for Adults*. He has researched a range of issues relating to classroom behaviour and, through his books, has equipped teachers to remain calm and deal with inappropriate behaviour.

Understanding Pupil Behaviour

Classroom management techniques for teachers

Ramon (Rom) Lewis

Routledge
Taylor & Francis Group

LONDON AND NEW YORK

First published by ACER Press, an imprint of
Australian Council *for* Educational Research Ltd in 2008

This edition published 2009
by Routledge
2 Park Square, Milton Park, Abingdon, Oxon OX14 4RN

Simultaneously published in the USA and Canada
by Routledge
270 Madison Avenue, New York, NY 10016

Routledge is an imprint of the Taylor and Francis Group, an informa business

© 2009 Ramon (Rom) Lewis

Typeset by RefineCatch Limited, Bungay, Suffolk
Printed and bound in Great Britain by CPI Antony Rowe, Chippenham,
Wiltshire

British Library Cataloguing in publication Data
A catalogue record for this book is available from the British Library

Library of Congress Cataloging in Publication Data
Lewis, R.
Understanding pupil behaviour: classroom management techniques for
teachers/Ramon (Rom) Lewis.
p.cm.
Includes bibliographical references and index.
1. Classroom management. 2. Problem children--Behaviour modification.
I. Title.
LB3013.L49 2009
371.102'4--dc22
2008029465

ISBN 10: 0-415-48352-2 (hbk)
ISBN 10: 0-415-48353-0 (pbk)
ISBN 10: 0-203-83391-8 (ebk)

ISBN 13: 978-0-415-48352-0 (hbk)
ISBN 13: 978-0-415-48353-7 (pbk)
ISBN 13: 978-0-203-88391-4 (ebk)

Contents

Acknowledgements

Thanks are due to Dr Joel Roache, Ms Helen Neville and Mrs Elisa Allan for their assistance in helping prepare this manuscript.

1 | Introduction

Background

For the last 20 years I have been working in a number of countries with groups of up to 115 teachers at a time, developing programs designed to instruct them in how to help their pupils behave more responsibly in class. I have provided sessions for at least ten such groups a year; consequently, over that period I have interacted with at least 10 000 teachers. One of the many issues these teachers discuss is whether pupils are becoming increasingly difficult to manage in schools.

To encourage reflection, I outline an authoritarian society in which one group is elevated and given the right and responsibility to control the behaviour of another. Historically this has meant that men controlled women, whites controlled blacks, employers controlled employees, adults controlled children and finally, teachers controlled pupils. I then ask the extent to which teachers agree or disagree that there has been a collapse of the authoritarian system in classrooms, with a corresponding deterioration in pupil behaviour and diminishing of respect for teachers and their authority.

Recently, more teachers have been saying that increasing numbers of parents and pupils are questioning their management decisions. It is no longer surprising for a Principal to receive a phone call from the parent of a child who has just been sent from the classroom and told to go to the Principal's office, before said child even arrives at the office. These days, pupils are seen by teachers as more likely to question or demand justification for teachers' judgments, and to refuse to cooperate with requests they see as 'unfair'. A recent example concerns 'Jason'.

Jason was sent to the Deputy Principal (DP) by a classroom teacher for talking repeatedly and arguing with the teacher. On receiving him, the DP said, 'Jason, sit over there please, as there is something I need to do before we can discuss what happened.' 'It's OK, I'll stand,' said Jason. The DP repeated quietly, 'Jason, I'll be a minute, so please sit over there. You're blocking the corridor.' 'It's OK, I'll stand,' replied Jason. Approaching Jason, leaning slightly towards him, looking strongly into his eyes and pointing to a seat, the DP said firmly, 'Jason, sit over there!' 'It's OK, I'll stand,' said Jason just as firmly. Moving even closer, the Deputy Principal responded loudly, 'I said sit over there!' 'And I said, I'll stand,' Jason countered.

You can guess what happened next. The DP could be heard three streets away as he yelled angrily at Jason, calling him names and demanding that he do what he was told. It's interesting to analyse this situation. Did the DP set his alarm the night before this incident thinking, 'I must get a good night's sleep so tomorrow I have plenty of energy to blast Jason in full view of at least five other school staff'? I don't think so. When the DP spoke to me regarding the incident, he said how Jason *made* him angry. He never intended to yell. However, that means that Jason not only controlled an adult, he controlled a DP. Such power can be addictive. He will probably be back.

It is not always something as dramatic as a confrontation of this type that leads to teachers being controlled by pupils. Recently, I was invited to a non-government girls' secondary college to conduct professional development sessions. I asked some of the teachers why they felt it necessary to invest one day of the staff's time in professional development in classroom management. They told me that some of the girls were doing things they never used to. On asking what it was that they were doing, a teacher stated that a girl sometimes said, 'No, I don't want to!'

At the time I was a little bemused, because the previous day I had given professional development sessions at a school where pupils had smashed the Principal's plate glass windows and written obscenities on the walls of the office. The pupils there also customarily told staff to go and ... have relationships, procreate or whatever. Nevertheless, for the staff at the girls' school, public resistance was uncommon and therefore not something with which they had had a lot of experience. Consequently, it was seen as challenging, and too often provoked a less than professional response from teachers. Between schools, there is substantial variation in what 'sets off' teachers.

This variation has also been noted in cross-national comparisons. In a study of classroom misbehaviour and management in Australia, China and Israel, my colleagues and I found that 'even though Chinese teachers report as much "misbehaviour" in class as do Australian and Israeli teachers, the nature of the misbehaviour in Chinese classrooms may be less extreme' (Lewis, Romi, Qui and Katz, 2005, p. 12).

The term 'misbehaviour' may be misleading. In truth, there are few types of behaviour that are 'bad' in all situations – even killing is not frowned on in times of war. Consequently, although 'misbehaviour' will be used at times in this book, 'inappropriate behaviour' is probably more accurate. Misbehaviour is not 'off target' as far as the pupil exhibiting it is concerned. Although it may be distracting, disruptive or disrespectful, the behaviour is often inappropriate only from the teacher's perspective. As far as the misbehaving pupil is concerned, the behaviour is very much on target as it serves a purpose and meets a need. In most cases, the need is related strongly to a context. For example, a pupil who acts inappropriately, given that the focus of classrooms is learning, may be feeling bored, uninterested, excited, or even threatened.

The way in which many pupils provoke teachers is not by swearing at them or openly challenging them. Often their inappropriate behaviour takes the form of simply ignoring the teacher or quietly resisting the teacher's attempts to manage them.

One recent example was typical. I was observing a teacher give an English class. I had done so a number of times and the pupils were already used to my presence. I observed two pupils (Jennifer and Deb) talking when they should have been listening. The teacher also saw it and told Deb, who was in the middle of speaking, to be quiet. Deb pretended not to hear, so the teacher repeated her demand in a louder voice. Deb then turned to the teacher and said that she had almost finished and it would just take a second. The teacher began to explain how Deb's talking was interfering with the other children's opportunity to hear. Halfway through her explanation, Jennifer, who had been taking part in the original conversation, said something to Deb, who then totally ignored the teacher, turned to her friend and continued the conversation. Naturally, the teacher was not amused, nor did she remain calm.

Some more experienced teachers find pupils' provocative behaviour to be more stressful than do younger teachers. The main reason for this is that, historically, they had dealt with such behaviour by assertively demanding compliance – much like the DP's approach to Jason described above. The trouble is, they never thought of their management techniques as techniques. It was more a case of who they were. When the techniques worked, they 'worked'. That is, they were competent teachers. They were OK.

Now that the same technique no longer works, it means that they are incompetent. They are no longer OK. It is not just a case of 'my techniques aren't working, what else can I try?' It is more akin to a crisis in psyche. The need for confidence regarding the impact of particular strategies is important to teachers given that the ability to manage pupils effectively is a critical component of their professional identity (McCormick and Shi, 1999). So critical is it that 'disciplinarian' ranks third, after 'leader' and 'knowledge dispenser', among the metaphors teachers give for their work (Goddard, 2000).

Authoritarian, democratic or what?

Teachers are not saying that all pupils reject the idea that teachers have the right and responsibility to manage the classroom behaviour of pupils. It seems, however, that the proportion rejecting this notion is increasing. In the words of a teacher at one of my professional development sessions, 'many pupils know all about their rights but don't seem to know much about how to act responsibly'.

It is not surprising that teachers are noticing that pupils seem more aware of their rights than their responsibilities. A study that examined the codes of pupil conduct of approximately 300 schools found that nearly all codes referred to the rights of pupils, and the majority of schools associated rights with responsibilities. However, a substantial minority (40%) made no such connection. There would appear to be an opportunity for a far greater emphasis on the link between rights and responsibilities (Lewis, 1999a).

Teachers, among others, have been instrumental in alerting pupils to their rights. According to theorists such as Maurice Balson, teachers have responded to a shift in community values by becoming more democratic in their outlook. For example, Balson (1992, p. 124) argues that in more authoritarian days:

> The roles of both teacher and student were clearly defined as those of superior and inferior respectively and each knew what was expected of the other in each situation. With the weakening of the authoritarian system and the strengthening of democratic processes, the vertical continuum of superiority–inferiority gave way to a system of social equality, a relationship which respected the rights of individuals to decide for themselves rather than being imposed upon.

It looks as if this is the case in Australia, as all states have abolished corporal punishment and generally officially encourage parent and pupil participation in the formulation of school management policies (Slee, 1988). After reviewing the policies of three Australian states, Balson (1992, pp. 2–3) concludes: 'It is clear that government policy guidelines are advocating, and taking firm steps in implementing, a democratic style of leadership in schools.'

However, while the rhetoric is that teachers have abolished or are changing from authoritarian relationships to democratic ones, and there appears to be a shift from more authoritarian to more democratic practices in classrooms, this observation is not sufficient to justify the conclusion that teachers have replaced their authoritarian beliefs with democratic ones. In my opinion, the reality is very different from the rhetoric, and this difference partly explains my reasons for writing this book.

Less authoritarian practices or more democratic ones?

It seems apparent that there are fewer authoritarian practices in schools today than there were 50 years ago. Why? Two alternative explanations are illustrated by an example from women's liberation.

Fifty years ago, if a woman had a career it generally ran a poor second to her husband's. It would be rare for her to spend substantial amounts of time outside the home to advance her career if it meant her husband would have to look after the children. Childcare was viewed as a woman's job. These days that is far less likely. One could argue that men have reflected on the nature of their relationship with women and the rights of women, and have concluded that women are their equals and should be treated as such.

Alternatively, it is possible to argue that any change in the power distribution between men and women has been brought about by the latter's unwillingness to be dominated as they once were. Consequently, men may have found that if they wish to be the dominant, or even a functioning, partner in a relationship they have to be more skilled and subtle in the way they go about it, giving a little bit of ground here and there in order to maintain their overall position.

The same arguments can also explain what may be currently happening in our classrooms. Perhaps teachers have been moved to revalue the rights of pupils and as a result are treating them in more democratic ways. Or perhaps it is as Balson (1992, pp. 5–6) argues:

> Beginning with the Black Power movement, there was a series of similar social revolts including women's liberation, the student power movement, and the industrial power movement. All had in common a refusal by the traditionally inferior group to accept a position of inferiority. Teachers found that they could no longer dominate students, while parents, males, whites and management found a similar resistance whenever they attempted to impose their values on children, females, coloureds and labour respectively.

My professional contact with teachers and consultants leads me to conclude that in many cases teachers are feeling forced to adopt a less authoritarian and more democratic style. Teachers say things like 'pupils know their rights, they won't let you order them, and they question everything'. When they talk about why they negotiate with pupils or allow them to participate in classroom decision-making it is often represented as a case of 'have to' rather than 'want to'. This attitude seems to be more common among secondary teachers than primary (elementary).

It is interesting to observe the way that teachers can unintentionally encourage pupils to resist their authority. They provide verbal and non-verbal cues that they don't expect to be taken seriously as an authority in the classroom.

A common verbal sequence can sound like the following:

> *T:* Excuse me, Ahmud, are you talking again? Didn't I speak to you about talking a few minutes ago? Are you ever going to listen to me? How many times do I have to tell you?

Obviously these questions were not meant to be answered, although contemplating likely answers can be informative.

> *T:* Excuse me, Ahmud, are you talking again?
>
> *A:* Of course, you wouldn't be speaking to me now if I weren't.
>
> *T:* Didn't I speak to you about talking a few minutes ago?
>
> *A:* Of course. What's the matter? Got a memory like a goldfish? Going senile, sir?
>
> *T:* Are you ever going to listen to me?
>
> *A:* It depends. What are you going to do if I don't?
>
> *T:* How many times do I have to tell you?'
>
> *A:* Hard one, Sir. How about 17? Twenty-three?

For the more challenging pupils such teacher questions reveal an under-assertiveness on the part of the teacher that is quickly recognised. The equivalent non-verbal situation relates to teachers standing side on and leaning away when giving long-winded assertive statements. Challenging pupils often have trouble with more than four words in a row, but, being somewhat visual in their learning style, very quickly size up the teacher who is defensive and who appears almost 'on the run'.

In summary, many teachers seem to be seeking control techniques that work. They are as interested in assertive techniques such as those of Lee and Marlene Canter (1996), or to a lesser extent Bill Rogers (1992), as they are in the more democratic practices advocated by William Glasser (1969) and Balson (1992). If these teachers have to negotiate with pupils or punish them to stay in control, they will. If they have to allow pupils more say in determining class rules, or bribe them, they will. They appear willing to adopt democratic processes, but largely for authoritarian purposes.

The Post-Guru Syndrome

Many teachers using or supporting democratic techniques do not appear to have reflected on the rights of pupils, or to have concluded that pupils have a right to be treated more like equals. Likewise, teachers opting for a more assertive approach to classroom management do not seem to have reflected at length on the appropriateness of the associated techniques or on the learning theory on which the techniques are based. Teachers appear to be interested only in their efficiency. This is a major problem and helps to explain what I call the Post-Guru Syndrome, or PGS.

PGS strikes school staff somewhere between two weeks and six months after a well-known management guru has visited the school and convincingly demonstrated how children should be managed. He or she is an expert and has a ready answer for all questions. Because of their knowledge, commitment, and charisma, gurus are extremely impressive. In many cases, they can not only say what to do, but can also demonstrate it in classrooms. Their tricks appear to work perfectly. Nevertheless, after teachers implement these new techniques it is often only a short time before they become inconsistent in the implementation of them, and finally falter. At this point, the teachers frequently feel more powerless and despairing than they did before the guru's visit.

> PGS strikes staff between two weeks and six months after a well-known management guru had visited the school and convincingly demonstrated how children should be managed … It is often only a short time before teachers become inconsistent in the implementation of the techniques, and finally falter.

It is interesting to reflect on a report by Lawrence Ingvarson (2005) that identified factors affecting the impact of professional development programs on teachers' knowledge, practice, pupil outcomes, and efficacy. He reported that, in general, one-day teacher professional development interventions have little overall long-term effect. It is my untested assumption that his conclusion is due to the different sorts of impact such days have on more effective and less effective teachers respectively. Teachers who are feeling competent and confident come away from guru-led days with a number of new and useful techniques, which they successfully integrate into their toolbox. On the other hand, if a teacher is struggling, any adoption of new practices is short-lived, leading to the syndrome described above. In summary, while some teachers improve their effectiveness, for others, it is reduced. Therefore, as noted by Ingvarson (2005), on average there is no overall positive impact on pupil behaviour and teachers' management skills.

The general inability of management interventions to bring about a change in pupil behaviour has also been noted in the research literature. In Australia, Hart, Wearing and Conn (1995) evaluated the impact of a $1.25 million staff development program, called the Whole School Approach to Discipline and Student Welfare Program. Their evaluation involved the collection of data from over 4000 teachers in 86 schools. They reported that over the 12-month period that schools were involved in the intervention, there was significant improvement in management policies. However there was no corresponding change in the mean level of pupil on-task behaviour in classrooms.

On a personal level, I recall working with the staff of a secondary school. After a series of professional development sessions, these staff learnt how to deal with inappropriate behaviour assertively, slowly and steadily meeting any resistance or repeated offence with a more serious sanction. They also learnt how to actively catch children being good and reward such behaviour. Finally, they were shown how to defuse developing power struggles with pupils and to calmly offer them choices of behaving reasonably or accepting the consequences, meeting with them if necessary to explain their actions. After three weeks, the principal of the school rang me excitedly to say how the staff members were commenting on their calmness and control. She also said that some pupils had approached her and said something like, 'what have you done to the teachers? They're nicer.' Nevertheless, less than a month later she rang requesting further professional development as teachers had regressed and were once again yelling at pupils.

The phenomenon of Post-Guru Syndrome can be further understood in the light of research on the role of metacognition in education (McInerney and McInerney, 2002; White and Gunstone, 1992). The area of metacognition, or 'thinking about one's thinking', is being pursued by a group of researchers who are attempting to explain the difficulties inherent in making permanent changes to an individual's ways of understanding the world. Although their work began in the area of science learning in secondary schools, the theory they propose is appropriate in explaining the effects of PGS. In doing so, it illuminates one of the major reasons for the gap between theory and practice highlighted earlier.

According to proponents of metacognition, learners develop schemata or frameworks for dealing with their knowledge or observations. In many cases these schemata are inconsistent with the state of knowledge in a given discipline and are therefore technically incorrect. When this occurs, the learners are usually given a description of the correct paradigm, and if they are fortunate, they are also told why their thinking is incorrect. Thus learners may frequently adopt a new schema, and may even be able to apply it consistently, without discarding the old, which is only temporarily suppressed. However, if the original schema is retained, it may eventually resurface and reassert itself.

To permanently change a given learner's schema it is essential for them to reflect on the paradigm they currently hold and find it unsatisfactory in the light of new information or observations. They then need to adapt their view, act in the light of that adaptation, and judge their new behaviour as satisfactory. If this isn't done, any modification made will most probably be temporary.

Applying these notions to PGS, it can be argued that the nature of many staff development activities precludes the sort of reflection required for a permanent shift in teachers' paradigms. During professional development sessions, teachers are often exposed for only a short time to very convincing gurus, who through a process of 'show and tell' demonstrate the effectiveness of a particular approach to classroom management.

Unless encouraged to do otherwise, teachers may focus on classroom techniques rather than on the assumptions on which they are based, since it is the techniques that appear to be of greatest relevance. Consequently, they may not reflect on the underlying learning theories associated with the differing models of classroom management.

These teachers may appear to have come to terms with assumptions about the potential of children (for example the extent of their intellectual and moral development) and the nature of self-discipline that underlie different approaches to classroom management. Nevertheless, their commitment to the assumptions behind a particular model of classroom management may be superficial at best. They may be able to temporarily suppress their views about children's potential to share power, and the ideal nature of teacher–pupil relationships, in order to adopt those of the guru. They may even appear to believe in, and defend, the guru's implicit theory.

Within a short time, however, their commitment to both the techniques and, more particularly, the related assumptions will be tested by pupil behaviour that appears inconsistent with the sort of response predicted by the approach. These pupil responses may be due to teachers' inability to replicate exactly the behaviour of the guru, or may indicate the limitations of the approach. Regardless of the reason, such unexpected pupil reactions can be viewed as quite threatening to teachers who thought they had it all worked out. In the face of such 'threatening' behaviour, it is likely that teachers may become even more inconsistent, or unrepresentative of the approach, and the 'problem' will escalate.

To limit the extent of perceived threat, teachers need to be very confident that the approach they are attempting to implement is worthwhile, and is likely to work in the long term. To feel this confidence, they need to have faith in the assumptions that support the approach. These vary, and in some cases contradict each other. Without a clear understanding of, and strong commitment to, the assumptions that underpin particular approaches to classroom management, it is unlikely that a teacher will persist in its implementation in the face of its apparent inadequacies.

The next step

The observations outlined above have encouraged me to adopt, adapt, and heavily augment much of what I included in the second edition of *The Discipline Dilemma* (Lewis, 1997b). In the first edition (1991), I refrained from discussing my own theoretical or practical orientations to classroom management, preferring to allow the reader to use the material provided to develop his or her own approach. In the second edition, I clarified my support for more democratic processes, without highlighting the use of specific techniques in any particular sequence.

Since completing the second edition, I have gained a lot more experience in providing professional development in schools. I am more conscious of many teachers' immediate need for a system of management capable of efficiently providing order in their classrooms, while promoting appropriate pupil values. I believe it will be useful, therefore, to present what I think is a comprehensive, coherent and apparently very acceptable and successful approach for teachers and schools that wish to help their pupils act more responsibly.

> Classroom management not only provides sufficient order to allow the teaching of 'reading, writing and 'rithmetic'. It also teaches values.

This approach assumes that it is not enough to skill up teachers in classroom management techniques. It is also necessary to set up support processes capable of facilitating an ongoing commitment by staff to productive management interactions with pupils, particularly those who are more challenging. It also assumes that classroom management not only provides sufficient order to allow the teaching of 'reading, writing and 'rithmetic'. It also teaches values.

Classroom management and pupils' values

It seems increasingly important for teachers and school administrators to understand fully that every interaction between teachers and pupils is a 'learning' experience for the pupils who are involved in it, or who witness it. Values are influenced. The significant role that teachers play in developing appropriate values in their pupils is recognised internationally. The interest of some commentators is stimulated by a concern over a perceived decline in pupil values (Lickona, 1996) and behaviour (Bennett, 1988; Houston, 1998).

For others, their interest stems from a belief that 'preparing good citizens, not higher test scores, has historically been the most important purpose of our public education system' (Rothstein, 2000, p. 419). For example, the last time the question of the relative importance of various goals of schooling was put to the American community via the Phi Delta Kappa Polls of the public's attitudes towards the public schools was in the year 2000. The function of schooling selected as the most important in that survey was 'to prepare people to become responsible citizens' (Rose and Gallup, 2000, p. 47).

In general, interest in pupil responsibility is expressed in two distinct but overlapping ways. The first emphasises pupils' morals, character and values (Fenstermacher, 2001; Hansen, 2001; Jones and Stoodley, 1999; Pring, 2000). The second focus of those interested in the character of youth emphasises civics and citizenship education (McDonnell, 1998; Osler and Starkey, 2001; Pearl and Knight, 1998).

Within each camp, there are also two divisions. Some see the area of value, moral character or citizenship education as a separate part of curriculum, added to, and augmenting, the 'normal' curriculum. Others argue that it is intrinsic to all aspects of the curriculum. For example, according to Richard Pring (2001, p. 110), 'Picking out citizenship as a subject in its own right fails to see that all teaching, when conceived as a moral practice concerned with values and conceptions of what it is to be human, necessarily is a preparation for citizenship.' As a result of being exposed to citizenship curriculum, pupils are expected to develop personal character traits, such as respecting individual worth and human dignity, empathy, respect for the law, being informed about public issues, critical mindedness and willingness to express points of view, listen, negotiate and compromise (for example Curriculum Corporation, 1997, p. 7). However, civics education programmes focusing on knowledge transmission alone have limited effect. The values that are to be promoted have to be incorporated into the day-to-day experience of pupils.

If we want greater understanding in civics, then pupils need the opportunity to engage, which in turn promotes their belief and understanding that participation and engagement are worthwhile (Mellor, Kennedy and Greenwood, 2001).

Independent of the civics debate, interest is also high with regard to values. A 2003 study on values education in Australia, funded by the Federal Government, focused on what values our children should learn, where and in what context they should learn them, and what role schools should play in their formation. The study found a number of examples of how values can be taught to pupils in both state and private schools (Zbar, Brown, Bereznicki and Hooper, 2003, p. 11). The values highlighted were caring, empathy and tolerance; peace and non-violence; respect, love, excellence, achievement and honesty; truth, fairness and integrity (p. 44).

The most common values identified for schools to consider were tolerance and understanding; respect, responsibility, social justice; excellence; care, inclusion and trust; honesty, freedom and being ethical (pp. 158–63).

Schools have always taught values and always will, but they vary in how directly they attempt to do this. Some do it by default, allowing the words and actions of staff and pupils to incidentally define what is important and what is not. Some teach values as an 'add-on' to the main curriculum (such as by emphasising and teaching the virtue of the month). Some take a more holistic approach and allow particular value positions to permeate their subject matter, whether it is Science, Maths or English. Others try to teach values using the 'hidden' curriculum, including things such as the pictures that are placed on the walls or the layout of the play areas (Ainley, Batten, Collins, and Withers, 1998; Thomas, 2000). Recent work in Australia identifies nine values of significance to Australian schooling:

1. Care and compassion
2. Doing your best
3. Fair go
4. Freedom
5. Honesty and trustworthiness
6. Integrity
7. Respect
8. Responsibility
9. Understanding, tolerance and inclusion.

(Commonwealth of Australia, 2005)

Classroom management interactions are integral to pupils' understandings of a number of these values, including responsibility, tolerance, care and concern for others, respect and honesty.

Those responsible for choosing approaches to classroom management ... have to understand the sorts of values and beliefs likely to be transmitted to pupils who experience or witness these different styles of management. Such values are not haphazard but are consistent with the assumptions underlying the different approaches.

Because values are so influenced by teachers' interactions with misbehaving pupils, those responsible for choosing approaches to classroom management need to consider carefully not just the efficiency of classroom management tricks or techniques described in books such as this one. They also have to understand the sorts of values and beliefs likely to be transmitted to pupils who experience or witness these different styles of management. Such values are not haphazard but are consistent with the assumptions underlying the different approaches.

In general terms, though, none of the values implicit in the approach to management outlined in this book would be unacceptable to school communities in a western democratic society.

Stress and classroom management

As indicated earlier, classroom management is a well-documented source of teacher stress (DeRobbio and Iwanicki, 1996; Friedman, 1995, 2006; Keiper and Busselle, 1996). It consistently rates as among the strongest of teacher stressors. Sometimes it is called classroom management, sometimes discipline, and sometimes relationships with pupils. Regardless of the label, it is a perceived inability to develop a good working relationship with pupils that both beginning and experienced teachers identify as a major cause of stress (Veenman, Voeten, and Lem, 1987).

Teachers stress when they feel unable to maintain an atmosphere in which pupils can get on with their work and teachers can teach without unnecessary interruption. It is not surprising, then, that any failure on a teacher's part to satisfactorily manage the classroom misbehaviour of pupils can result in stress, and in extreme cases, burnout. Nevertheless, it needs to be noted that some stress-related results may be tenuous because teachers experiencing stress as a result of other factors (such as excessive workload) may perceive pupil behaviour more negatively (Whiteman, Young and Fisher, 1985) and therefore inflate its significance as a stressor. Regardless, management issues rate consistently among the strongest of teacher stressors, both locally and internationally.

> Teachers stress when they feel unable to maintain an atmosphere in which pupils can get on with their work and teachers can teach without unnecessary interruption.

David Chan (1998), reporting on the stressors of over 400 teachers in Hong Kong, notes that pupil behaviour management rates as the second most important factor stressing teachers. More significantly, perhaps, Richard Ingersoll (2001) studied approximately 6700 teachers in the United States and says that approximately 30 per cent of the 400 or so who choose to leave the profession identify pupil management as one of the reasons that caused them to give up teaching. An earlier study in Western Australia also noted that for many Australian teachers the stress associated with classroom management was cited as a reason for resigning from the profession (Bruce and Cacioppe, 1989).

It is common for the popular press to sensationalise the 'problem' of classroom misbehaviour and the associated teacher stress. For example, articles entitled 'Safety of teachers must come first', 'Critical delay on "bad kid" classes', or 'Counsellors needed for school discipline crisis' appear to suggest that school misbehaviour threatens both teachers and pupils. However, inspection of many reports of pupil misbehaviour does not indicate the presence of a very significant problem (Fields, 1986; Hart, Wearing and Conn, 1995; Oswald, Johnson and Whittington, 1997). Similarly, research on teacher stress and concern levels show that they are best described as moderate (IEU, 1996; Pithers and Soden, 1998).

Research reporting on misbehaviour and teachers' levels of concern over management issues in classrooms in China, Israel and Australia (Lewis *et al.*, 2005) shows that approximately two-thirds of teachers report that 'in the first class they will teach next week', they expect 'hardly any' or 'none' of their pupils to misbehave. When asked in that study 'to what extent is the issue of classroom management and pupil misbehaviour an issue of concern to you?', most reported that it is no more than a minor stressor, about a quarter said moderate and approximately 10 per cent stated that management is a major source of stress. In summary, although it can be seen that there is little support for the view that there is a *crisis* in classroom management, over a third of Australian teachers appear to be experiencing at least moderate levels of stress resulting from pupil misbehaviour.

As stated earlier, since 1984 I have spent many hours in a professional capacity as an adviser talking with groups of teachers about issues of management. These teachers had sought information on the topic because they were concerned about it. Many were frustrated because they spent hours developing what they believed were exciting and relevant lessons only to have pupil misbehaviour destroy the experience for all. Others had very little difficulty dealing with all but a small minority of pupils whom they found extremely challenging, due to these pupils' confrontational behaviour and apparent lack of respect for them. Not all were concerned about their lack of control, however. Some were able to maintain order in the classroom but felt that far too much time was being 'lost' in classroom management.

In addition to professional development experience with teachers, and an awareness of relevant research literature, there is one other major reason why I am convinced that the matter of classroom management and relationships with pupils can be a very stressful part of teaching. Although I am not permitted to name the schools at which I have taught, I can say that they were not easy ones in which to establish order in the classroom. I have no doubt that schoolteachers need to concern themselves with the unacceptable behaviour of pupils. Nevertheless, given the relatively straightforward nature of most stress-inducing pupil behaviours, I am confident that the approach to management highlighted in this book will, if utilised consistently, increase pupil responsibility and substantially reduce teacher stress.

Having discussed the central role of classroom management in the process of schooling and some of the problems associated with it, Chapter 2 will focus on teacher aggression towards pupils and its negative impact on both pupils and teachers. The remainder of the book will outline what can be done to assist teachers to use more productive disciplinary strategies. There are two aspects to the solution offered. The first centres on classroom management techniques able to be used with pupils displaying different patterns of misbehaviour. These are techniques capable of meeting not only the need for order in classrooms but also the need to create responsible citizens. These are discussed in Chapters 3 to 7. This is followed by Chapter 8, which provides research support for the techniques recommended. The second part of a solution to the problem of pupils controlling teachers focuses on how to set up a process of teacher support capable of ensuring that teachers do not regress. This process is the focus of Chapter 9.

2 | Teachers' aggression towards misbehaving pupils

Disciplinary techniques used by teachers

I recently wrote (Lewis, 2006) a comprehensive review of Australian research into the ways that pupils see primary and secondary teachers dealing with classroom behaviour. It shows that primary teachers frequently encourage their pupils to participate in rule formation, hint that behaviour should improve, and praise and reward appropriate behaviour. They often hold discussions with pupils about the inappropriateness of misbehaviour and punish pupils who misbehave, increasing the level of consequence if pupils argue or repeat the misbehaviour. Primary teachers are rarely considered to have acted aggressively by humiliating pupils or acting unfairly.

> Secondary teachers appear to frequently hint and punish, only sometimes recognise appropriate behaviour and have discussions with pupils, and hardly ever involve pupils in decision-making.

Secondary teachers appear to frequently hint and punish, only sometimes recognise appropriate behaviour and have discussions with pupils, and hardly ever involve pupils in decision-making. Nevertheless, 'both primary and secondary teachers are seen, at least sometimes, to yell angrily at pupils who misbehave and to keep a class in because some students misbehave' (Lewis, 2001, p. 312).

Four categories of pupil behaviour

To understand these findings more fully, it is instructive to consider four categories of pupil behaviour (labelled Category A, B, C and D respectively). This delineation underlies the discussion of management techniques in Chapters 3 to 5, and provides the basis for the structure of this book.

Pupils who manifest behaviours characteristic of the first category (Category A) generally respond appropriately to the curriculum and undertake whatever work the teacher gives them. These children usually seem to assume that the work is important enough to attempt, and easy enough to be mastered. Such pupils respond to 'hints' such as a teacher pausing, moving closer, inspecting the child's work or saying that there is a problem.

Pupils whose behaviour places them in the second group (Category B) are less interested in the work and may be less confident of their ability to complete it. Consequently, they are occasionally distracted and can sometimes be distracting. The behaviour of these children often improves as a result of a teacher's judicious use of recognition and rewards, as well as punishment.

The third category of behaviour (Category C) comprises actions sufficiently challenging to warrant a pupil's occasional isolation within the class or removal from the classroom. When such pupils are isolated, the teacher usually provides an opportunity for a 'chat'. During this discussion, the teacher helps the pupils become aware of the unreasonable impact their behaviour has on other pupils. Once the child acknowledges that the behaviour is a problem, a plan or contract is developed for avoiding repetition of such unreasonable behaviour in the future. Although one chat will normally not be sufficient, after a number of these chats, pupils who display Category C behaviour usually move to behaviour characteristic of Categories B or A.

The final type of behaviour (Category D) involves repeated misbehaviour despite a teacher's use of all of the above techniques.

Although some pupils' behaviour will remain firmly within one of the four categories (A–D), it is likely that others will show behaviour patterns reflecting more than one category. The frequency and type of misbehaviour can often be related to what is being learnt and how it is being taught. When pupils are feeling competent and can see the relevance of the work they are doing they are more likely to display behaviour typical of Categories A or B.

However, when they are less interested in the work or feel that they are unable to achieve, then it is possible they can move to Category C-type behaviour. Pupils displaying behaviour characteristic of Category D can be helped to improve only if radical improvement occurs in their self-concept.

It is extremely important to understand that I am not offering a fixed and permanent way of categorising pupils. In contrast, I am arguing that at particular times, in particular contexts, pupils can display characteristic patterns of behaviour. If handled in an appropriate manner, pupils can be assisted to improve their behaviour. Therefore, if a teacher effectively identifies the type, frequency and goal of misbehaviour, and provides the sort of classroom management pupils need (depending on whether their current patterns of behaviour reflect those of Category D, C, B or A), pupils can all develop Category A behaviour. In this way, they all will become highly responsible, and learning opportunities of all kinds will be maximised.

Five kinds of power

To provide a theoretical framework for interpreting how teachers attempt to gain responsible behaviour from all pupils, I am going to refer briefly to a theory of power developed by John French and Bertram Raven (1959). This analysis of power in relationships continues to provide a valuable form of scaffolding for those examining classroom discipline (Tauber, 2007).

In dealing with the misbehaviour of pupils, teachers may knowingly or unknowingly draw upon five kinds of power:

1. Coercive power is the power a teacher has over a pupil stemming from the pupil's desire to avoid punishment associated with inappropriate classroom behaviour.
2. Reward power is the power related to a pupil's desire to gain something they want. Teachers who provide the desired recognitions and rewards for appropriate behaviour have such power.
3. Legitimate power is the power that is inherent in the role occupied by teachers, bestowed upon them by society, coming with the position they occupy.
4. Referent (or relationship) power is the power that pupils give to teachers whose relationships they value. It stems from respect for, or liking of, the teacher. Teachers with Referent power are trusted by pupils, as friends are trusted.
5. Expert power stems from a pupil's belief that the teacher has the ability to pass on important knowledge and skills, and they will gain something valuable if they cooperate.

The findings reported earlier that secondary teachers very often use hints and assertive strategies to respond to classroom misbehaviour probably arise because such strategies meet the needs of pupils displaying Category A and B behaviour, discussed above. Since teachers on average report that only some of their pupils misbehave, A and B pupils form the majority of pupils in most classrooms. Although teachers could use one-on-one discussions before giving out punishments such as isolation and detention, it appears that this kind of response to misbehaviour may be reserved for pupils who are unwilling to respond to the teacher's Legitimate, Coercive or Reward power.

It needs to be noted, though, that Reward power is not readily offered to individual pupils. It may be argued that it is only when the application of Legitimate power and Reward power is ignored or resisted that teachers adopt strategies based primarily on Referent power, and try to change pupils from the inside out rather than from the outside in.

Primary teachers, however, appear to rely more heavily on Referent and Reward power than Coercive, and arguably value more highly their relationship with pupils.

Frequency of teachers' aggressive behaviour

Despite the unproductive nature of aggressive teacher responses to the inappropriate behaviour of pupils, quite a few teachers appear to be using such techniques. In Australia, for example, both primary and secondary teachers are seen, at least sometimes, to yell angrily at pupils who misbehave and to impose detention on classes because some pupils misbehave.

> 62% of secondary students and 68% of elementary students indicate that their teachers at least sometimes yell in anger at students who misbehave. In addition, 42% of secondary and 35% of elementary respondents report that their teachers at least sometimes use sarcasm, and 30% and 19% respectively report the use of putdowns. Finally, 45% and 60% of secondary and elementary teachers respectively are seen to at least sometimes keep the class in because some students misbehave. These figures are substantial and a cause for concern. (Lewis, 2006, p. 1199)

Why teachers use aggressive classroom management techniques

During a study leave year from my university, I returned to teaching full-time as a teacher of science and maths in a secondary school. I had a colleague, whom I shall call Mr Edwards. He was suffering a great deal of stress from teaching. It was not because he didn't know his subject; he knew it very well. His problem was classroom management and it culminated in a change of schools at the end of the year.

The problem appeared to me to be partly provoked by Mr Edwards himself. I became aware that he was screaming at his pupils, occasionally

> I became aware that he was screaming at his pupils, occasionally using abusive language and sarcasm, and frequently using group punishments like class detentions ... In his calmer moments it was clear that he even liked the same pupils he abused in class.

using abusive language and sarcasm, and frequently using group punishments like class detentions. In conversations, however, Mr Edwards clearly indicated that he was aware of the negative impact such techniques might have on a teacher's relationship with pupils. It was not that he didn't care about his pupils and their right to be treated respectfully; he did. In his calmer moments it was clear that he even liked the same pupils he abused in class.

I was not surprised by Mr Edwards' behaviour because I had chanced upon it a number of times previously with other teachers. On many occasions, during professional development sessions on 'discipline' at their schools, members of staff would tell me privately that to keep a class under control they were forced to do things that they felt very uncomfortable about. Mostly they spoke of uncontrolled yelling on their part, as well as sarcasm and group punishment.

To gather some systematic information on the views teachers hold on the use of hostile management techniques, I conducted two studies. In the first, I taped hour-long interviews with 20 teachers from ten secondary schools. Two teachers from each school were recommended by their principals on the basis that they appeared to operate very different models of classroom management, one teacher relying on Legitimate and Coercive power and the other emphasisng Referent and Reward power. With the exception of two teachers, all interviewees expressed a desire to avoid techniques that could harm pupils psychologically.

The following quotations, each taken from a different interviewee, represent typical responses:

I try not to [make pupils feel less able or worth less], but at times, I'm sure it does.

I try very hard not to use [anger or belittling of pupils] because of the effect that it might have.

Well, I don't like yelling, because I don't think yelling is very productive and I don't like being yelled at myself ... and I don't like making any of the kids feel rotten.

I certainly wouldn't want to apply negative psychological impact.

I don't like putting kids, anyone, down. I'm sure I do it sometimes, but it is something that I would try to avoid.

The two dissenters were of the view that:

> If … a child's behaviour was affecting the other pupils, I wouldn't really hesitate to have some sort of negative effect on them, for the benefit of the others, because there are 20 or 21 kids in a class.

Despite their general desire not to use sarcasm or display anger towards pupils, all the teachers interviewed acknowledged that they did in fact do these things. Many suggested that they were very cautious and used it only on pupils who required it and whom they thought probably wouldn't be affected by it.

Some typical responses were:

> I would only occasionally do that [use sarcasm] and I would be very careful which kid I chose … some kids are just not able to accept it, to take it.

> I try to bring a kid down if it's the right kid, to give them a dressing down.

> It's only the very timid and shy pupils that would really shiver at it [anger], I think.

> Some of the other well-behaved kids you would destroy, but the kids who don't behave, I think you'd find it very difficult to have a negative effect on them completely.

The ripple effect of hostility

If these teachers were correct in assuming that a targeted pupil could withstand the use of sarcasm and anger without it having a great effect, it remains to be explained why so many pupils state a strong preference for teachers to avoid these techniques (Lewis, 2006). It appears that a 'ripple effect', noted by Jacob Kounin (1970), is in operation. That is, a teacher's behaviour towards one pupil has an impact on 'non-target' pupils.

> There are some kids that are really bad and they seem to go out of their way to annoy the teacher … their joy in life is to annoy the teachers … I use sarcasm to get rid of them … then I can concentrate on the kids that want to learn.

The teachers interviewed did not appear to be aware of this possibility. The response of one particular interviewee provides a dramatic example. In the early part of the interview the teacher stated:

> I think every kid's different. You've got to really treat each kid differently. There are some kids that are really bad and they seem to go out of their way to annoy the teacher. They are not interested in their work or

lessons, their joy in life is to annoy the teachers … and I do use sarcasm … I use sarcasm to get rid of them. I send them to the back of the class or even stand them outside the door, which you're not supposed to do. But then I can concentrate on the kids that want to learn.

However, this teacher later recounted the following story of his own schooldays:

Well, when I was at school I was very, very, quiet, I was very, very shy. I still am. I went to the Collingwood Technical School and the teachers there were very tough and if you didn't conform, they really got into you. I remember my mate in my Maths class and the teacher said – I forget his name – come out to the blackboard and do this equation.

And this poor kid couldn't do it, and wow, the teacher bawled him out in front of the class. His mind must have been a blank I suppose and he's doing algebra on the blackboard, and he couldn't do a thing, and this teacher was tearing him to shreds, and I'm thinking … Oh my God, he's going to ask me next, and I'll die.

The story is particularly relevant because the teacher suggested that he had been a well-behaved pupil who was rarely punished.

In addition to this ripple effect of sarcasm on the bystanders in a classroom, there is the possibility that some pupils (those showing Category C and D behaviour) are not scared by the teacher's use of sarcasm but are excited or angered by it. Such pupils are also likely to be distracted from their work, but not because they are worried that the teacher might be sarcastic to them. On the contrary, they would welcome the opportunity to give the teacher what he or she deserves. They don't sit and shake, they sit and mentally rehearse the hostile response they plan to make if the teacher is stupid enough to choose them as the next target.

When the four groups of behaviour described above (Categories A–D) are considered, it becomes obvious that in classes where more pupils display Category C and D behaviour, they are more likely to promote and witness greater teacher aggression towards pupils behaving inappropriately. However, pupils showing Category C and D behaviour patterns are precisely those who are least likely to respond well to such provocation.

Teachers who lose their tempers and yell at such pupils, or attempt to quell their misbehaviour by using cutting sarcasm, are likely to escalate the conflict. The fact that these teachers generally have a genuine regard for their pupils and a desire to avoid such counterproductive techniques does not prevent them from doing things they regret. Why, then, does it happen?

Theories that explain teacher 'misbehaviour'

There are three competing yet interrelated theoretical explanations for teachers' misbehaviour towards challenging pupils. Each is plausible.

Attribution theory

The first of the possible explanations for a teacher's use of aggressive disciplinary techniques is attribution theory (the 'no one can be expected to cope with these kinds of kids' response). This approach is based on attribution theory as developed by Fritz Heider (1958), Edward Jones and Keith Davis (1965) and Harold H. Kelley (1973), and Bernard Weiner's attributional theory of achievement motivation (1985, 1994). The idea is that teachers may use aggressive techniques with such children because kids like this don't and can't be expected to understand, appreciate or respond to more reasonable classroom management techniques. The reasons are typically seen to reside in the pupils' natures or upbringing.

Consequently, when a pupil exhibits challenging behaviour that teachers find confronting they may respond by giving the pupil what 'kids of this kind' deserve. According to this explanation, pupils who deny a teacher's legitimate authority and act in a way which they clearly understand is irresponsible and unfair, deserve (maybe, need) to be put in their place. Any resistance justifies an angry response from the teacher. In addition, any class that acts irresponsibly deserves to be punished as a group. Even if some pupils were not directly involved in the misbehaviour, they didn't try to prevent it.

Efficacy theory

The second theoretical explanation for a teacher's use of aggressive discipline techniques relates to low levels of perceived self-efficacy (the 'I'm hopeless at this' response). This view is based on Albert Bandura's theory of self-efficacy (1994). Within this conceptualisation, when teachers view their resources (emotional and professional) as inadequate to deal with the management situation they confront, they feel incompetent and unable to cope.

Francis Fuller and Oliver Bown (1975) provide some insight into the relevance of efficacy theory to the question of why sensible teachers occasionally do counterproductive things to pupils they like. First, they postulate that the things that concern (and stress) teachers generally change as a teacher gains more experience and self-confidence. Initially, teachers have concerns about themselves. The questions that dominate are along the lines of: will I look right? can I appear knowledgeable? and so on.

However, once teachers realise that they have the personal characteristics required to occupy the role of a teacher, there is a movement from concerns about the self to concerns about the task of teaching: how do I question? what is an efficient way to explain a concept? It is only when these concerns are allayed, as teachers become competent in and confident about their teaching abilities, that the next level of concern is reached. It is at this third level that teachers become fully aware of and concerned about what is best for *pupils*, for example what style of interaction and what sort of content best suit individual pupils.

The second aspect of Fuller and Bown's model relevant to explaining a teacher's aggressive behaviour towards pupils is as follows. Teachers who have graduated from focusing on concerns about themselves and the task, and who are mainly occupied with ways of designing instruction most relevant to pupils' needs, will regress whenever they feel very threatened or insecure. That is, when confronted by a situation they perceive as very stressful, teachers may move from focusing on what is best for pupils to being relatively more concerned about their own needs. At these times, they will act to protect themselves even if it is at the expense of pupils.

There is a second way in which efficacy theory can explain teachers' use of aggressive disciplinary techniques. Some teachers may choose such strategies because they see it as in the interests of all (including the misbehaving pupil) to suppress misbehaviour in a manner they perceive as extremely efficient. Sarcasm, for example, can quickly shut down many pupils. So can yelling in anger.

Attachment theory

The third of the dominant potential theoretical explanations for a teacher's aggressive and unproductive responses to challenging pupils is based on attachment theory (Bowlby, 1975, 1981, 1982).

A teacher's feelings of rejection and hurt, related to the perceived unfairness of the behaviour of a challenging pupil, promote an emotional withdrawal and often an aggressive response from the teacher. This 'stuff them' reaction from teachers is thought to stem from insecure styles of attachment. Such teachers may be unable to respond to young people with affection or support, be unable to trust them, or may need and want emotional support from their pupils and be unable to cope with apparent rejection.

Imagine an extremely dedicated mathematics teacher. For this teacher the study of mathematics is one of the most significant pursuits in the world. She devotes many hours to lesson preparation, working late into the night, to ensure that her next lesson is interesting, relevant and as engaging as possible. Through such a captivating lesson she knows she will gain great admiration from her pupils. However, when she presents her 'baby' to the class, a particularly challenging pupil destroys the process she worked so hard to develop. He not only rejects her baby, but also destroys it. The extreme sense of rejection and hurt she experiences may cause her to react very aggressively.

A study that can shed some light on explanations for teachers' use of aggressive management techniques is a survey of 507 primary and secondary teachers in Australia (Lewis, 2004).

Teachers indicated how often they used techniques such as:

- yell angrily at pupils who misbehave
- keep a class in because some pupils misbehave
- make sarcastic comments to pupils who misbehave, etc.

They then reported why they did these things. There were no statistically significant differences between the support for alternative reasons provided by primary and secondary staff. The reasons most commonly selected by teachers were:

I do it because I'm frustrated.

It allows the lesson to continue.

It makes the pupil listen to me.

It puts me back in control.

Between 40 and 61 per cent of teachers agreed or strongly agreed that these were reasons that explained their aggressive disciplinary behaviour. These findings suggest support for efficacy theory. In contrast, the reasons least likely to be selected as relevant were:

If I don't, the pupil won't learn to behave properly.

It makes me feel better.

The pupil deserves it for behaving so badly.

Only 20 per cent of teachers agreed or strongly agreed with each of these reasons. Consequently, there appears less support for both attribution and attachment theory. However, much more work is required before the contribution of the competing theories can be fully appreciated.

Teachers' self-defeating attitudes

Since efficacy theory appears most relevant to explaining teachers' unproductive treatment of challenging pupils, a brief analysis of teachers' attitudes is useful. Michael Bernard (1990) has written extensively on how the level of stress associated with feelings of inadequacy depends to some extent on a teacher's attitude. He concludes that because teachers can modify their counterproductive attitudes, the level of threat can be reduced.

The counterproductive or, as Bernard calls them, *irrational* attitudes are generally extreme and out of touch with reality. Imagine a teacher who believes that *all* of his or her pupils *have* to do as they are told *all* of the time. This teacher also believes that successful teachers *should* be able to control their pupils' behaviour completely – and it would be *really awful* if even one pupil didn't behave as requested. Further, assume that this teacher believes he or she *needs* to be in charge to avoid being a failure, not only as a teacher but also as a person. When confronted with inappropriate behaviour, any teacher maintaining these sorts of attitudes is going to be very highly stressed. Relatively serious misbehaviour may be seen as truly awful – a catastrophe that cannot be tolerated.

It is likely that a teacher with such extreme attitudes would feel very threatened if confronted by, for example, a class clown. This is because attention-seekers are as interested in the reactions of the rest of the class to their behaviour as they are in the reaction of the teacher. Therefore, they may not immediately, or even ultimately, do as they are told. Similarly, a pupil who frequently makes unnecessarily disrespectful challenges to a teacher's authority may also offer too much of a challenge for any teacher with less rational attitudes.

In reaction to inappropriate pupil behaviour, less rational teachers frequently respond by labelling the pupils as hopeless, or rotten to the core. Moreover, they may readily regress to being concerned about their own survival and willingly deny the pupils' rights if it means protecting themselves. It is very unlikely that these teachers would calmly and consciously react in a professional way, selecting an appropriate response from the range of acceptable alternatives, keeping in mind the needs of the individual pupil. An aggressive response is much more likely.

If such teachers were more in touch with reality, they would recognise that it is not possible to make pupils do what they are told all of the time. Sometimes pupils are feeling frustrated, angry, embarrassed, depressed, or are experiencing some other negative emotion, and do not respond logically. A more rational attitude for a teacher to hold would run along the following lines: 'I would *prefer* that I were able to manage the behaviour of all my pupils and that they did as they were told, and I will try to find techniques to achieve my aim. But if a pupil refuses to cooperate, I can manage to live through the situation while I continue to seek a strategy that works.'

However, as the research reported in this chapter has shown, despite all attempts to keep cool, the most rational teacher occasionally 'loses it' and acts aggressively towards misbehaving pupils. The question that needs to be asked is: when they do, what effect does it have on pupils?

The impact of teachers' aggressive classroom management

There is a substantial body of research from recent decades (see Lewis *et al.*, 2005, 2007) showing that the use of aggressive strategies in the classroom is non-productive. This includes observational studies (e.g. Gottfredson, Karweit and Gottfredson, 1989; Kounin, 1970) and surveys of teachers, pupils and parents (e.g. Hyman and Snook, 2000; Lewis, 2001).

Results have shown that where teachers verbally abuse children, humiliate them by the use of sarcasm, frequently and repeatedly exit them from class, or impose arbitrary and harsh punishments, children can experience a range of short-term and long-term negative consequences. These include less interest in the subjects being taught (Henderson, Fisher and Fraser, 2000), absences from school, withdrawal or suspension, and an increase in high-risk behaviours such as smoking and drug or alcohol abuse (Piekarska, 2000; Sava, 2002). Studies have shown that 15-year-olds absent from school have higher levels of psychopathology (Borg, 1992), and engage in more frequent high-risk behaviours (Handelsman and Gupta,

> Where teachers verbally abuse children, humiliate them by the use of sarcasm, frequently and repeatedly exit them from class, or impose arbitrary and harsh punishments, children can experience a range of short-term and long-term negative consequences.

1997). Disengagement from schooling, frequent referrals out of class, absences from school or exclusion have a significant impact on future opportunities for education or access to employment.

The negative impact of teachers' aggressive classroom management techniques on pupils has been known for many years. A study I was involved with approximately 20 years ago concluded:

> Students who are less able to concentrate on their school work, and who are more likely to think less positively of their teacher after their teacher handles misbehaviour in their classroom, are likely to perceive more of the following teacher behaviours: mistargeting, either by the teacher choosing the wrong student or by blaming the sins of individuals on the group; showing anger and, in the case of students' attitudes to their teacher, not providing clear and rational rules; using arbitrary or unreasonable sanctions and moving students without warning. Once again, teachers perceived as more supportive of appropriate classroom behaviour are associated with more positive student attitudes. (Lewis and Lovegrove, 1987a, p. 183)

Furthermore, two other studies of pupils' reports of their teachers' disciplinary behaviour and their attitudes to the subject taught by that teacher concluded that pupils may become less interested in subjects taught by teachers who display anger, mistarget and punish innocent pupils, and don't give warnings before issuing punishments. This occurs even though the importance attached to the subject is not affected (Lewis and Lovegrove, 1988).

These results appear very consistent with those of Darrell Fisher, Barry Fraser and others who, in a series of studies, demonstrated that pupils who perceived their teachers as admonishing and strict were those with less interest in the subject being taught (e.g. Fisher, Henderson and Fraser, 1997; Henderson, Fisher and Fraser, 2000).

A replication of the earlier studies, Lewis (2001), examined the views of over 4000 secondary pupils and almost 600 pupils in primary schools. Once again, teacher aggression is associated with more pupil dislike of the teacher and greater distraction from schoolwork.

Given the observations reported earlier, that the majority of pupils see their teachers as at least sometimes providing aggressive responses to misbehaving pupils, it is not surprising that secondary pupils are at least 'some of the time' distracted by their teachers' classroom management strategies and as often feel annoyed at a teacher when he or she deals with misbehaviour. This is despite the observation that 'more than sometimes' they think the teachers' intervention was necessary. Primary pupils report about the same level of negative affect as the secondary pupils, but more distraction, even though they are more likely to see the teacher's interventions as justified.

It is of interest to recall that in one early study (Lewis and Lovegrove, 1987b), which examined Year 9 pupils' reaction to management, the proportions of pupils 'more than sometimes' distracted, seeing the teacher's behaviour as unjustified and feeling negative towards the teacher were 35, 42 and 42 per cent respectively. The corresponding figures for the same year level, almost 20 years later, are 39, 49 and 32 per cent. For primary pupils the recently reported proportions are 48, 51 and 38 per cent. It is of interest to note that the corresponding figures for pupils in Israel and China are similar (Lewis, Romi, Qui, and Katz, 2007).

Consequently, there does not appear to be a great deal of difference in secondary pupils' reaction to management over time, although in more recent times secondary teachers appear less likely to be thought of more negatively for implementing disciplinary strategies. In general, these proportions are very substantial and indicate that many pupils are adversely affected by witnessing or experiencing the way their teachers handle pupils' misbehaviour in classrooms (Lewis, 2007).

As stated earlier, most teachers are quite aware of the need to minimise disciplinary techniques that distract pupils from their learning, and to use these techniques infrequently at most. Even teachers who don't resort to aggressive techniques still appear to have concerns about the disciplinary techniques they do use. In general, their ideas of best discipline practice involves significantly more empowerment of pupils than is currently the case in their classrooms (Lewis, 1999b; Lewis and Burman, 2006).

It appears that teachers want to decrease their dependence on a search for pupil obedience and to increase their reliance on approaches that are more inclusive of the voices of pupils. Put in terms of power, they seek to reduce Legitimate and Coercive power and increase their reliance on Referent and Reward power (Lewis and Burman, 2006). Such a position would appear to be consistent with the increasing interest in the earlier reported relationship between schooling and the development of appropriate citizenship attitudes and skills.

The tension between current and preferred management practice is generally not of great concern to teachers, although those for whom the gap is largest report the most stress (Lewis, 1999b). It is, however, of interest to reflect on how teachers attempt to cope when their disciplinary techniques are more authoritarian than they would wish.

Teachers' coping strategies

According to Samuel Green and Margaret Ross (1996: 315), 'only a few studies have been devoted to understanding the coping strategies used by teachers'. This position is reinforced by Chan (1998: 146): 'research studies on teachers' job-related coping behaviour and on coping as a mediator between teacher stressors and distress have been comparatively neglected.'

Nevertheless, a 1999 study examined the coping behaviour of almost 300 teachers (Lewis, 1999b). This study reports that the most common responses of teachers to any stress associated with an inability to manage classrooms as they would like are to put more time into their work and to seek support from others. They also regularly reflect on a plan of action, while putting more effort into their relationships with others and making time for leisure activities. These strategies were used either 'many times' or 'almost every time' by approximately 50 per cent of teachers. There is occasional use of five other strategies: focusing on the positive, maintaining a sense of humour, playing sport, working on one's self-image, and attending relevant meetings. In general, between 24 and 35 per cent of teachers used these responses many times or almost every time.

> The most common responses of teachers to any stress associated with an inability to manage classrooms as they would like are to put more time into their work and to seek support from others.

The least commonly used strategies, with the exception of seeking professional help, are those that have been described elsewhere as 'dysfunctional' (Lewis and Frydenberg, 2004). Strategies in this group (such as worrying, letting off steam, ignoring the issue, blaming oneself, keeping concerns to oneself, wishful thinking, and getting sick) were used many times or almost every time by only 4–6 per cent of teachers. It can be concluded that teachers most commonly respond to concern about the gap between current and preferred classroom management practice with productive coping strategies.

However, greater teacher concern about an inability to manage classrooms as desired is associated with greater use of the range of dysfunctional coping responses listed above. These strategies were reported as used sometimes by approximately 20–30 per cent of teachers (Lewis, 1999b).

Surveys of teaching staff have shed interesting light on the way these strategies are implemented. During professional development sessions I conducted, secondary school staff said they would be cheerfully going about getting ready for school when suddenly they would realise that today was Thursday, and not Wednesday as they had thought. From then on the day was ruined by worrying about the fact that they now knew they faced the dreaded 10E that afternoon. Other staff spoke about waking at approximately 2 a.m. to worry about the way things went, or better, didn't go, in class the day before. While awake they would blame themselves for things they had said and felt they shouldn't have, or things they could have done that they didn't do. Some said that they did this at 2 a.m. while they ate comfort foods like chocolate or ice cream.

One of the best manifestations of wishful thinking I have heard came from a teacher who stated that she lay awake in the early hours of the morning wishing that her dreaded 'Matthew' would get hit by a bus. Not killed, just hospitalised. She'd even send work, and correct it. A couple of months would just about do (it was September at the time). A less dramatic version of wishful thinking was exemplified by a teacher who lived in the hope that one particular family in the school would move suburbs, taking their three very difficult children with them.

In summary, it appears that on average teachers generally cope productively with the stress of being less professional than they would want to be in the area of classroom management. The most useful strategies include dealing directly with the problem while staying socially connected, fit, and relaxed. They are far less likely to use strategies characterised as less productive, if not counterproductive, such as self-blame and ignoring the problem, and very unlikely to get sick in response to their concern.

It is also clear, however, that those teachers who are most stressed are more likely to use maladaptive strategies which may contribute to, or at least maintain, their high levels of stress. Rather than increase their range of problem-solving responses, they become less likely to share their concern, and increase their use of self-blame, wishful thinking, and so on. It seems that such dysfunctional strategies also undermine or negate the benefits that accrue from the use of more adaptive strategies such as being problem-focused and keeping fit and relaxed, as argued by Lewis and Frydenberg (2002).

> Those teachers who are most stressed are more likely to use maladaptive strategies which may contribute to, or at least maintain, their high levels of stress.

The more stressed teachers are also more likely to get sick in response to their concern. It is relevant to note that this occurs despite the fact that they are likely to use productive strategies as often as their less concerned peers. This outcome appears consistent with the observation of Chan (1998, p. 147), who argues that 'it is recognized that not all coping strategies are likely to reduce distress and that certain coping strategies such as avoidance … may even exacerbate distress'.

It is ironic to combine knowledge about teachers' coping with the idea of Post-Guru Syndrome discussed earlier. According to PGS, many teachers who cannot sustain the techniques displayed by a guru fall back on techniques they would rather avoid. As a result, they become more concerned about the realisation that they are not disciplining pupils in a manner they would want. These teachers are those most likely to use self-damaging coping responses. One could almost argue that as far as they are concerned, it might be kinder to keep the gurus out of schools.

Having sketched the problems, what remains is to explain how they might be addressed.

3 | Developmental management in the classroom

As has already been explained, there are, at any time, four different patterns of pupil behaviour in classrooms. Category A behaviour is generally displayed by children who respond appropriately to the curriculum and undertake whatever work the teacher gives them. Category B behaviour shows a pattern whereby the pupil is occasionally distracted and sometimes distracting. Category C, on the other hand, comprises kinds of misbehaviour, and levels of persistence, sufficient to warrant a pupil's occasional isolation within, or removal from, the class. The final category of behaviour, Category D, is one where pupil misbehaviour seems to occur repeatedly despite teachers' best efforts. The classroom management techniques to be described in the following chapters are based on the assumption that teachers will only become aware of which pupils are displaying which patterns of behaviour by initially treating them as if they are all in Category A.

For shorthand purposes, throughout the remainder of this text, categories will be applied to pupils manifesting A, B, C or D patterns of behaviour. That is, I will speak of Category A pupils or Category D pupils, and so on. The risk here is that you may come to think of pupils as residing permanently in a category. This is not the case. These categories are to be used as a way of identifying the most appropriate management strategies for a respective pupil. The aim of doing that is to move pupils efficiently from Category D to C, to B, to A, at which time all pupils will be acting responsibly. Hence the use of the term 'developmental management'.

It is sometimes difficult to pinpoint which pupils, as a result of their behaviour, should be placed in which categories. I can recall conducting a discussion with all the teachers of a particularly challenging Year 8 class at a secondary school. As we discussed the behaviour of individual pupils it seemed as if the behaviour of nine of the 24 pupils indicated Category D. Subsequent experience showed it to be four. Since then I have found that, with only one exception, all 'difficult' classes with which I have been asked to help have had no more than four pupils manifesting Category D behaviour. What seems to be happening, however, is that teachers can unwittingly provoke pupils at Category C, and sometimes even Category B, to act like those at Category D. Before moving into a discussion of managing inappropriate behaviour, in whatever category it appears, it is useful to focus briefly on how to stimulate appropriate behaviour, so that misbehaviour is minimised.

What causes inappropriate behaviour?

Views about the causes of a pupil's inappropriate classroom behaviour can be placed along a continuum. At one end is the belief that the behaviour has to do entirely with some deficiency in the pupil. The assumption is that pupils only behave inappropriately because there is something wrong with them. This explanation, commonly referred to as a deficit model, highlights the pupil's problematic psychological make-up, or sociological factors which contribute to his or her lack of conformity.

Under the deficit model, solving problems associated with a child's lack of conformity involves a variety of approaches ranging from exercising control over the pupil's behaviour, to counselling.

> The assumption is that pupils only behave inappropriately because there is something wrong with them … [Another belief] proposes that if pupils behave unacceptably, it is entirely the fault of the curriculum.

At the other end of the continuum is the belief that the child's lack of conformity is an expression of genuine and justifiable dissatisfaction with an educational institution that fails to cater for his or her legitimate needs. It proposes that if pupils behave unacceptably, it is entirely the fault of the curriculum. Either the material being covered is not seen as sufficiently relevant or interesting, or the process of instruction is not stimulating enough to maintain the interest and attention of pupils. This view focuses on solutions that require institutional changes to curriculum content and processes, timetabling, resources, staff–pupil relationships and pupil–pupil relationships (Greaves, 1987).

A nice way to clarify the distinction between the approaches is by using a simple analogy, that of the proverbial square peg in a round hole. According to the first explanation, if there's any difficulty fitting a square peg (the pupil) into the round hole (the school setting), then the teacher has to concentrate on whittling the edges off the peg. According to the second explanation, the peg's shape is fine and it is the shape of the hole that must be adjusted.

The only proponents of either extreme of this continuum seem to be theorists. Most experienced teachers recognise that a pupil's inappropriate behaviour results from a combination of both factors.

To some extent, teacher responses to pupils' inappropriate behaviour can be considered independently of changes to curriculum content and process. It is largely this view that underlies the approach to discipline presented in the remainder of this book. Nevertheless, the content and process of the instruction offered by teachers is clearly relevant to the appropriateness of the classroom behaviour of all pupils, although it is probably most relevant for those in Categories C and D. Before focusing on how teachers can usefully respond to inappropriate classroom behaviour, therefore, I will give some attention to ways in which teachers can reduce the likelihood of it occurring in their classroom.

Avoiding disruption

Since the early 1970s, there has been a growing body of literature surrounding the work of Kounin (1970). He analysed videotapes of teaching to identify the sorts of things teachers did that were associated with pupil disruption. He labelled some of these variables quite strangely, using terms like 'dangles', 'flip flops' and 'thrusts'; however, the concepts behind these terms are familiar to experienced teachers. According to Kounin, there are a number of features which consistently characterise classrooms where little time is lost because of inappropriate behaviour. These features can be summarised under four headings: keeping the lesson flowing smoothly; keeping pupils interested; keeping pupils accountable for their learning; and making pupils feel monitored.

Keeping the lesson flowing

To keep a lesson flowing smoothly there are some things that should be done and some that should be avoided. Among the former are the following:

- Know exactly what you are going to do and have all the necessary resources ready.
- At the beginning of a lesson and of a topic, inform the pupils about the aims of the instruction and the activities they are going to do to achieve them.
- Whenever possible, set up an accepted and fully understood pattern for pupil behaviour so that time is not repeatedly lost in negotiating with pupils (e.g. toilet passes, distribution of materials, roll-taking, lining up).
- Let pupils know when an activity is about to be changed so they can prepare to finish what they are doing and mentally get ready for what is about to begin.

- Always attend to the needs of the majority of the class and have them engaged in learning before dealing with individual pupils who require special attention.
- In introducing a new task, give clear directions. Specify why the task is being done, how it connects to work already completed or about to be undertaken, what is to be done, and an approximate time limit for the activity. Allow pupils time to seek clarification before setting them to work.
- Give all instructions before beginning work so you don't have to interrupt the pupils with more instructions once they have started.

Having completed the do's, it is useful to consider some of the most important don'ts:

- Don't spend more time on any activity than is required (e.g. handing out equipment, explaining, or telling a pupil off).
- Don't interrupt a discussion on one topic to jump to a different one even if you later return to and complete the first topic. (For example, halfway through discussing the answer to question 4, you remember that you forgot to tell the pupils some important information about the answer to question 3. Don't interrupt yourself. Finish off your answer to question 4, then return to question 3 and complete it. Then you can proceed to question 5.)
- Don't allow yourself to be sidetracked into answering irrelevant questions or requests. This is particularly important when a new activity is being initiated.

Keeping pupils interested

A pupil's interest in learning can be stimulated and maintained in a number of different ways:

- Vary the volume, speed and tone of your voice.
- Be enthusiastic about what you teach (e.g. whenever possible say why it is useful, important, interesting and/or exciting).
- Vary the manner in which you teach. This includes using a variety of procedures such as assignments, debates, excursions, guest speakers. Variability also relates to individual lessons, which should include techniques that cater for a range of learning styles (Lazear, 1999), such as teacher explanation; teacher–pupil discussion; role plays; pupil–pupil discussion in small or large groups; individual pupil seatwork; and the use of media (e.g. films, videos, the overhead projector, data display, interactive whiteboard, posters, objects). It is important, however, to ensure that the selection of a particular process is based on its appropriateness to achieving a particular objective.
- Move around the room while teaching and allow pupils to move occasionally.
- Ensure that the lesson content is challenging but achievable, and whenever possible relevant to the interests of pupils.

Keeping pupils accountable for learning

Pupils who feel that the teacher is both concerned about how much work they do and prepared to check up on them are less likely to behave inappropriately.

The following are some of the ways in which accountability is manifested in the classroom:

- When questioning a class, don't accept the first correct answer and move on; take a number of answers before saying whether they are correct.
- Frequently, ask a question and then try to make eye contact with as many pupils as possible before selecting a respondent.
- After asking a question and nominating a respondent, be prepared to wait a little time (say five seconds) until the nominated pupil begins to answer.
- If a pupil has given an inadequate answer, taking into account the ability of the pupil, wait up to five seconds to encourage him or her to continue the answer.
- Occasionally ask a pupil who has given a correct answer why he or she decided on the answer.
- On some occasions, have all pupils jot down onto scrap paper answers to all questions asked of the class. Then move around the room and read out some answers.
- Collect and/or correct all homework set.

Making pupils feel monitored

This final feature, identified by Kounin as a characteristic of teachers who keep the inappropriate behaviour of pupils to a minimum, is the ability to have 'eyes in the back of your head'. Some of the ways teachers communicate this myth are as follows:

- Whenever possible, position yourself in the classroom so that by lifting your eyes you can see all or most of the classroom. For example, when addressing a class, position yourself at a corner of the room. That way all pupils are within a 90 degree sweep of your eyes. If you teach from the centre at the front of the room, surveying an entire class requires a sweep of almost 180 degrees.
- When talking with one pupil, do not become oblivious to the rest of the class. Frequently 'break' eye contact to scan the rest of the pupils (approximately every five seconds). Whenever a pupil is seen to be off-task, inform him or her that the behaviour has been seen and is not acceptable. This need not be done publicly, that is, across the room. The message may be delivered privately at another time. The important thing is that the pupil knows that any inappropriate behaviour will be quickly picked up by the teacher.

Obviously, to discuss adequately what constitutes good teaching would require much more than a few pages. Further, it is obvious that I have almost ignored curriculum content. This is not because the latter is unimportant or irrelevant to a discussion on avoiding inappropriate classroom behaviour, but because it is a much more contentious issue and therefore cannot be satisfactorily dealt with in a cursory way. Nevertheless, it would be inexcusable to avoid the discussion entirely since there is solid evidence that good teaching reduces the likelihood of unacceptable pupil behaviour.

The pile of goodwill

In addition to very specific processes like those already mentioned, there is one much more general aspect of good teaching. It is critical to the avoidance and handling of inappropriate classroom behaviour. I call it 'maintaining a pile of goodwill', which is a less technical way of saying maintain Referent Power (see Chapter 2). It is those pupils who display behaviour characteristic of Categories C and D who stand to gain most from teacher goodwill, as will be explained in Chapters 6 and 7.

Teacher–pupil interactions are not restricted to those in which the teacher intends to change some behaviour of the pupil that is seen as unacceptable. There are, one might hope, many other opportunities for contact between teacher and pupil. It is during such occasions that pupils develop their basic ideas about a teacher. Most significantly, they reach a decision about the degree of genuine concern that a teacher has for them and for their learning. It is within such a context that pupils interpret a teacher's use of management techniques.

Some teachers convey to pupils, in most of their interactions, that they see the children as some sort of animal or as dumb adults to be trusted only partially, or as lesser beings without dignity to be manipulated at will, or as identity-less entities to be filled with information. In such a situation, it is unlikely that management techniques will be successful. For example, a teacher who does not convey a sense of connection with and concern for a pupil is unlikely to engage that child in a meaningful problem-solving discussion, during which the child is meant to express freely his or her genuine concerns. Without trust in the teacher's motives, the pupil's involvement will be at best superficial. Similarly, if a teacher is 'coming on strong' in accordance with a more authoritarian view, most pupils are likely to resist if they believe that the teacher hasn't got their best interests at heart.

To build up a pile of goodwill on which to draw, you need to spend 'positive' time with pupils. This time is spent teaching them, listening to them and encouraging them. It also means recognising their strengths, helping

> To build up a pile of goodwill on which to draw, you need to spend 'positive' time with pupils. This time is spent teaching them, listening to them and encouraging them. It also means recognising their strengths, helping them, accepting their help, and putting yourself out for them.

them, accepting their help, and putting yourself out for them. This extends to such things as showing interest in their lives outside the classroom and the school, supporting their sporting interests, showing interest in their problems, and generally conveying to them that you respect, value and like them, and are genuinely interested in their welfare.

Estimating goodwill

To determine the size of your pile of goodwill with any particular pupil, you might ask yourself the following questions:

- When was the last time I did something nice for or to that child?
- When was the last time I spoke to the child in a friendly, supportive manner?
- How often have that pupil and I spent time together talking about something that is important to him or her?
- What is the pupil's favourite film, music, school activity, football team, sport, etc.?
- Who are the pupil's best friends, worst enemies, or casual acquaintances?
- What does the pupil think of his or her schoolwork and other teachers?
- What does the pupil feel he or she is really good at?
- What is the pupil really interested in?
- Does the pupil know I am aware of his or her competencies and interests?
- How often have I had the pupil help me in a meaningful way?

If you are unable to answer many of these questions it is likely that the main reason is your inability and/or lack of willingness to spend time with the pupils in question. Often the opportunities for teachers to explore these facets of a pupil's life are limited. For example, secondary teachers are often responsible for about 100 pupils daily. Furthermore, the teacher may spend time with some problem pupils only during a detention period, when the teacher may wish to be left alone to correct some tests or plan a lesson. They may even use this detention time to give the pupils a 'telling-off', damaging whatever goodwill they may have established.

When you know very little about a pupil's 'world' it is likely, although not necessarily the case, that your pile of goodwill is not as great as it could be, and in many cases should be. If, on the other hand, you have interacted with the pupil in a caring, concerned and interested manner so that the appropriate answers to the previous questions roll off your tongue, the chances are great that the pile of goodwill is sufficient to allow you to draw heavily on it when handling the pupil's inappropriate behaviour.

Although the need for a pile of goodwill will be obvious to some, many teachers are unwilling or unable to invest the energy required to earn a pupil's trust. In many cases the reason relates to whose needs are being met. As explained in Chapter 2, a teacher who feels threatened or rejected may use damaging sarcasm or call pupils names.

However, there are many far less extreme situations which inform pupils that a teacher is not concerned enough about what is best for them. For example, during seatwork, it is possible to have a quiet hum of working noise or attempt to get absolute silence. The former is more difficult for teachers because hums invariably increase in volume until they begin to sound like roars. Relative silence is easier to maintain because it's easier to recognise. Although the best interests of pupils may be served by having a low hum of working noise which indicates that pupils are helping each other (and pupils realise this), some teachers seek to protect their own interests at the expense of the pupils' by insisting on silence.

It is not always self-interest on the part of teachers that prevents them developing substantial piles of goodwill with their pupils. Teaching is a very stressful profession with many competing demands on a teacher's time. In addition to being required to teach, assess and report on more and more curriculum content, teachers have to find time for school administration. They also need to maintain the ongoing education necessary to keep up with advances in the material they teach and the most effective ways of teaching it. For many teachers there just does not seem to be enough time to take a personal interest in pupils.

Where there is little opportunity for pupils to feel recognised and respected, they may need to find ways of being noticed, and, as will be explained in Chapter 7, one way is to exhibit chronic attention-seeking behaviour. Consequently, teachers can spend a large amount of time in disciplining these Category D pupils, leaving even less opportunity to develop a pile of goodwill, and so the cycle continues.

As stated above, the level of goodwill between teachers and pupils can drop when teachers feel challenged or rejected. At such times they may resort to the use of Legitimate power ('You'll do what you're told!') or Coercive power ('If you don't stop, you're getting a detention!'). However, when this is done in the absence of Referent power (power based on your ability to develop a relationship) and Reward power, it doesn't work.

One might hypothesise that with classes of pupils more prone to misbehaviour, teachers would find more need to generate Reward power by recognising responsible behaviour, just as they find more need for Coercive power, comprising punishment and aggressive responses. However, a recent study which examined the way teachers treat classes containing more of the misbehaving pupils found that teachers not only failed to provide more recognition for appropriate behaviour, but also failed to generate the Referent power that can arise from having productive discussions with misbehaving pupils (Lewis, 2006, p. 1207).

The problem is that any teacher who applies Legitimate or Coercive power in the absence of a relationship with pupils runs the risk of making things worse. This is more likely if the child's behaviour is in Category C or D than if it is in Category A or B. How then does a teacher begin to help pupils to behave as responsibly as they are able? The answer is to design a management approach that minimises overt application of Legitimate and Coercive power while not omitting the application of Referent and Reward power. Such a management approach is outlined in Chapters 4 to 7.

Setting up expectations for appropriate behaviour

Generally, the way in which pupils are meant to behave in classrooms is enshrined in the idea of Rules. There is, however, a drawback to having rules, even 'fair' rules (Rogers, 2002). The idea of rules reeks of Legitimate power. Rules are things that a teacher (with or without class participation) creates to control the behaviour of pupils in Category B, C or D. For all Category A and most Category B pupils, rules have been useful and entirely acceptable. They provide the pupils with protection and little inconvenience. For pupils whose behaviour places them in Categories C and D, the situation is very different. Rules represent a negative experience associated with feelings of negation and control. The more difficult the pupils, the more likely they are to be provoked by the concept of rules.

> A teacher has to encourage pupils to understand that the main ... reason he or she attempts to alter or to stop certain pupil behaviour is because it interferes with the rights of other pupils.

If you shouldn't have rules, what then? The answer is – responsibilities attached to rights. A teacher has to encourage pupils to understand that the main, if not only, reason he or she attempts to alter or to stop certain pupil behaviour is because it interferes with the rights of other pupils. There are only two major rights to be protected.

The first is that all pupils have a right to learn as much as possible in classrooms. This is because schools are not malls. They are institutions of learning. As a consequence, teachers have a responsibility to ensure that no pupil is permitted to interfere with the learning of any other.

Ideally, assuming there are enough A and B pupils in the class, expectations for behaviour and all decisions related to classroom management should be handled during short classroom meetings. This is the name given to a regular meeting of all class members at which pupils establish and constantly evaluate expectations for behaviour, and discuss the good and bad aspects of classroom routines and members' behaviour. These meetings comprise all members of the class, and all (sometimes including the teacher) are given equal status and can raise issues and express their opinions and feelings. The meetings give pupils valuable opportunities to engage in a democratic decision-making process and provide a way of planning for change. A key aspect of such meetings is the search for consensus. According to theorists such as Rudolf Dreikurs and Pearl Cassel (1972), or Glasser (1986), such meetings should, in part, focus on setting expectations for appropriate pupil behaviour and solving 'discipline' problems. The meetings offer a way of establishing, among other things, definitions and understandings of rights and responsibilities in the classroom. In practice, such meetings are much more common in primary schools, where pupils are more likely to let teachers act as powerful agents of influence, than in secondary schools, where pupils are more likely to reject the guidance of teachers.

Both Glasser and Dreikurs assume that pupils are rational people who will learn, by experiencing the consequences of good and bad behavioural choices, to make good choices. They do not accept any excuses for inappropriate behaviour, regardless of whether the causes are attributed to conditions existing within school (e.g. boring teachers) or at home (e.g. broken families). Although teachers may understand the influence of these factors on pupils' patterns of behaviour they must never allow inappropriate behaviour to be acceptable.

Classroom meetings in practice

The introduction of classroom meetings in one of my Year 8 and Year 10 science classes was initially treated with suspicion by both the school administration and the pupils. The parents were informed of my intention to introduce a little more democracy into my science classes about two weeks before the first class meeting (about halfway through the school year). Although I offered to discuss with parents the reasons for introducing these democratic procedures, I was not contacted by any parent of the pupils in these two classes.

To prepare my pupils for the beginning of group decision-making I discussed with them the difference between what might usefully be called *rational* and *irrational* obedience. I argued that, in later life, people need to know how to participate in decision-making and obey with discretion, so that they do not give the responsibility for their own behaviour to someone else.

As part of this discussion, I referred to the methodology and results of a well-known experiment by Stanley Milgram (1975) in which the large majority of subjects in an experiment apparently electrocuted to death innocent people under the instruction of a supervisor simply because they were told to 'continue the experiment'. In addition, I indicated the general need of all members of a democratic society to know how to participate in group decision-making processes.

The first classroom meeting for Year 10 was somewhat weird. Despite my insistence that they needed to exercise self-control as a group, the first decision they took was to instruct me to be in charge. They said that as I had managed misbehaviour reasonably well for the last six months, I should continue to decide on appropriate classroom behaviour and act judiciously to see that appropriate behaviour occurred. The idea was that it was my responsibility, not theirs, to ensure order in the classroom. Using a democratic process, they used their empowerment to remove choice, not foster it. What was left for me to do? I, of course, pulled rank and ordered them to empower themselves.

Classroom rights and responsibilities

What does one do about setting expectations if the thought of a classroom meeting is too threatening? Recent research (Lewis and Burman, 2006) indicates that teachers want to provide more opportunity than they currently do for pupil voices to be heard, by way of classroom meetings. It is clear from this study that 'teachers perceive that constraints exist in schools which act to inhibit them from implementing their own ideas of best classroom management. The most significant of these appear to be heavy workload, lack of support from school administration, and class and classroom size' (p. 12).

In addition to accepting that pupils have the right to an opportunity to learn, the class also needs to recognise the right of all to feel safe (physically and emotionally) in the classroom. Teachers are obliged to protect pupils from any harassment by classmates. Once again, if pupils are a bit reticent it may be necessary to ask a direct question such as: 'Do you want me to do or say anything if a classmate attempts to physically hurt you or put you down?'

Having established the teacher's role in protecting pupils' rights, it is also imperative that pupils identify how *they* should or shouldn't behave if the rights of their classmates are to be respected. There are two aspects to this. The first is what they should or shouldn't do if they personally are to behave responsibly. This type of responsibility will be

Rights and Responsibilities in the classroom

In this classroom, pupils and the teacher have the right to do as much work as possible.

Therefore, their Personal responsibilities include:
- pupils should bring all their equipment to class;
- pupils should listen when other pupils are speaking;
- pupils should be on time;
- pupils should attempt all work; and
-
-

Their Communal responsibilities include:
- pupils should encourage others to bring all their equipment to class;
- pupils should encourage classmates to listen when other pupils are speaking;
- pupils should encourage others to be on time;
- pupils should encourage others to attempt all work; and
-
-

In this classroom: pupils and the teacher have the right to feel comfortable and safe.

Therefore, their Personal responsibilities include:
- pupils should pass all objects hand to hand;
- pupils should speak politely;
- pupils should keep their hands to themselves; and
-
-

Their Communal responsibilities include:
- pupils should encourage others to pass all objects hand to hand;
- pupils should encourage others to speak politely;
- pupils should encourage others to keep their hands to themselves; and
-
-

Understanding Pupil Behaviour Copyright © Lewis 2009

Figure 3.1   Pupils' rights and responsibilities

called Personal or Individual responsibility. The second is what they should try to encourage their classmates to do (or discourage them from doing) so that all pupils in the class act responsibly. For example, it is not enough for pupils to listen when other pupils are speaking. They should also see it as reasonable that they encourage their classmates to listen when pupils are speaking. That is, they should discourage friends from interrupting their classmates. This type of responsibility will be called Communal responsibility.

There is no need to compile a comprehensive list of responsibilities. It is enough to flesh out the idea. Figure 3.1 (page 43) outlines a typical outcome of such a discussion. Note that the list is not fully defined. There are unidentified expectations. The idea is that pupils should eventually be prepared to judge a situation and determine if their (or their classmate's) behaviour is responsible or fair. There are only two criteria: does it interfere with any pupil's right to feel safe, or their right to learn?

As was noted strongly in Chapter 1, classroom management aims not only to establish order but also to teach values. Hence, in a democratic culture, the idea that pupils should respect the rights of others is an essential learning outcome. The assumption that they should encourage others in their community to act responsibly is an objective that schools need to achieve. As explained earlier, it is only through experiential learning that pupils can be expected to assimilate a genuine respect for rights. What, then, can teachers do to see that their pupils protect such rights?

4 | Responding to pupils manifesting Category A behaviour

When dealing with pupils whose behaviour can be characterised as belonging to Category A, teachers need to draw on their Legitimate or Referent power. These powers are based on the understanding that teachers are officially designated to see that pupils' rights are protected, and that they are acting in the best interests of all the pupils in the class. Assuming that all pupils are in Category A implies that they may, at worst, only have to be reminded when their behaviour is preventing others from feeling comfortable or from learning effectively. They may also need to be made aware if they are not acting to help their peers behave in a way that is respectful of the rights of others.

> Legitimate and Referent powers are based on the understanding that teachers are officially designated to see that pupils' rights are protected, and that they are acting in the best interests of all the pupils in the class.

To make pupils aware that a 'problem' exists there are at least four kinds of verbal hints teachers could use. None of these *demand* anything from the pupil because, once Category A pupils realise a problem exists, they will modify their behaviour to become more responsible. Theorists such as Glasser (1986) and Thomas Gordon (1970) are proponents of such techniques. The observant reader may note that although hints don't demand compliance, the emotional pressure on a responsible pupil like those in Category A becomes increasingly compelling, as the examples below demonstrate.

It should be noted that before giving a verbal hint, it is assumed that teachers would have tried less disruptive, non-verbal hints. These might include pausing, moving closer to pupils or checking their work.

General hint

The first kind of hint is one that describes the situation in a general way. Some hints focus on the inappropriate behaviour in an attempt to stimulate pupils to stop it, whereas others emphasise the positive to encourage pupils to emulate classmates who are acting responsibly. Hinting can be directed both at Personal and at Communal responsibility.

For example, regardless of the specific nature of the inappropriate behaviour, a teacher could say to a class:

Positive focus (Personal responsibility):

> Some pupils are acting very responsibly.
>
> Just about everyone appears to be respecting their classmates' rights.

Negative focus (Personal responsibility):

> Some pupils are ignoring the rights of their friends.
>
> I see a pupil who is being unfair.

Positive focus (Communal responsibility):

> Some pupils seem willing to discourage their friends from ignoring the rights of other classmates.

Negative focus (Communal responsibility):

> Some pupils aren't encouraging their friends to behave responsibly.

Specific hint

The second kind of hint addresses specific behaviour but is still descriptive and doesn't present any demand. For example, if a teacher became aware that some pupils were finding it difficult to concentrate because of the noise, he or she might say:

Positive focus (Personal responsibility):

> It looks like most children are allowing others to hear.
>
> Only a few pupils are making it difficult for others to hear.

Negative focus (Personal responsibility):

> There is so much noise that some pupils can't hear my explanations.

I notice that there are some pupils who are finding it difficult to hear because of the noise.

Positive focus (Communal responsibility):

It looks like most children are trying to see that their classmates allow others to hear.

Negative focus (Communal responsibility):

Very few pupils seem willing to encourage others to reduce the noise, so that their classmates can hear the explanations.

Similarly, a teacher concerned about a pupil throwing a stapler to a friend might say:

Positive Focus (Personal responsibility):

Nearly all pupils are being careful when passing equipment.

Pupils are generally passing equipment in ways that keep us all safe.

Negative Focus (Personal responsibility):

Pupils are put at risk when things are thrown in the classroom.

I just saw a stapler thrown in the room. That's dangerous.

Positive Focus (Communal responsibility):

Some pupils seem willing to remind their friends to be careful when passing equipment.

Negative Focus (Communal responsibility):

I just saw a stapler thrown in the room. No one seemed worried about it.

Finally, if a teacher were concerned about harassment he or she might say:

Positive focus (Personal responsibility):

Pupils by and large seem to know how to treat each other respectfully.

I see that most pupils know how to be nice to their classmates.

Negative focus (Personal responsibility):

> Some pupils are talking disrespectfully to each other and someone's bound to get upset.

> Some pupils are scaring others because of the way they are treating them.

Positive Focus (Communal responsibility):

> I see that some of you are willing to help your friends be nice to classmates.

Negative focus (Communal responsibility):

> Pupils don't seem prepared to stop others from talking disrespectfully to their classmates.

Restatement of expectations

The third kind of hint focuses on re-emphasising the understanding shared within the class about what behaviour is responsible. For example, to encourage Category A pupils to communicate respectfully, teachers could say things like:

Positive Focus (Personal responsibility):

> We said that pupils should talk nicely to each other, didn't we?

> I thought that pupils were expected to let their classmates get on with their work, without interruption.

Negative focus (Personal responsibility):

> Didn't we agree that pupils wouldn't talk disrespectfully to each other?

> I thought that classmates' work was not to be interrupted.

Positive Focus (Communal responsibility):

> We said that all pupils should help their friends with the work.

Negative focus (Communal responsibility):

> We agreed that we all would stop others from talking disrespectfully to their classmates.

I-messages

The third kind of non-interventional statement is called an 'I-message' (Gordon, 1970). These statements indicate the nature of the problem, the behaviour that's causing the problem, and how the teacher is feeling about it. Once again, the message can be directed at Personal or Communal responsibility and focus on the negative or positive. For example, using the same situations as above a teacher may say:

> I-messages indicate the nature of the problem, the behaviour that's causing the problem, and how the teacher is feeling about it.

Positive focus (Personal responsibility):

I'm pleased to see that some pupils are waiting quietly to begin.

I'm relieved to see that pupils are treating each other nicely.

Negative focus (Personal responsibility):

I'm upset that some pupils talk during instruction because others miss out.

I get scared when things are thrown in the classroom. Someone could be seriously damaged.

Positive focus (Communal Responsibility):

It's good to see some pupils are prepared to stop their friends from throwing things in the classroom. Someone could have been hurt.

Negative focus (Communal Responsibility):

I'm disappointed that some pupils are allowing others to talk during instruction because others can't hear and won't know what to do.

Direct questions

Some other more interventional hints are phrased as questions. These are not addressed to the class but are asked of particular pupils. Examples addressing the same issues as above may be:

What are you doing?

What should you be doing?

Should you be talking now? Throwing a stapler? Speaking to your friend in that manner?

Are you behaving responsibly? Are you being fair? Are you encouraging your friends to be reasonable?

Verbal hinting in a classroom usually combines a number of the different types of hints above. For example, assume that a teacher is attempting to address the class and one or two small groups of pupils are still trying to complete the last activity and are therefore speaking among themselves. To hint, a teacher may say, 'I notice that not all groups are ready. It's a pity because if they continue to talk, some pupils won't hear the instructions. I'm disappointed that some of you didn't remind them to get ready.' Similarly, if a teacher has a number of latecomers enter after lunch she may say, 'It's good to see most of you got back in time. I'm also pleased because I noticed that some of you reminded your friends to come in. After all, we did agree that we would try to get as much work done as possible.'

Obviously all hinting assumes that the pupils are Category A and will correct their behaviour after the hint is given, even if it needs to be repeated a number of times. If pupils don't respond appropriately they are no longer considered Category A pupils, but their behaviour is now in Category B, C or D. Until proved otherwise, we will assume that any who show they are not in Category A are all in Category B! These pupils will form the focus of the next chapter.

To summarise, it is important to:

1. Establish expectations based on pupils' rights to learn and to be physically and emotionally safe.
2. Ensure that pupils articulate the need for the teacher to act to safeguard pupils' rights.
3. If possible, establish expectations for appropriate pupil behaviour through classroom meetings.
4. Let pupils know when they act in a way that is respectful of, or interferes with, pupils' rights.
5. Address the inappropriate behaviour of Category A pupils with verbal hints, namely:
   • General hints
   • Specific hints
   • Restatement of expectations
   • I-messages.
6. When hinting, consider whether to emphasise the behaviour you wish to encourage or discourage and whether the focus is Personal or Communal Responsibility.

5 | Responding to pupils manifesting Category B behaviour

Three types of power most relate to the treatment of pupils manifesting Category B behaviour. These are Legitimate (Role-related), Reward and Coercive (Punishment) power. The best-known proponents of a reward and punishment approach are Canter and Canter (1996), who developed and market Assertive Discipline.

Of the powers involved in this approach, the most potent is Reward. Reward power appears to increase a teacher's stock of goodwill, whereas the implementation of punishment decreases it.

> Teachers who use punishment more often are seen as more distracting when they respond to misbehaviour. Punishment also associates with secondary students' dislike of the teacher … The use of recognitions … associates with a more positive reaction towards the teacher and a greater belief that the teacher's interventions are necessary. (Lewis, 2006, p. 1206)

However, as argued above, when you provide recognition and reward for appropriate behaviour, particularly for that of difficult pupils, you need to demonstrate that it is the pupil's behaviour that is the focus of (although as explained later, not the reason for) the reward. A teacher who rewards pupils when they demonstrably respect the rights of classmates encourages the pupils to trust his or her motives. It is reasonable to expect that such teachers are more likely to be accepted when they need to deal with misbehaviour.

During my conversations with school staff at professional development sessions, many senior teachers have stated that when misbehaving pupils are sent to them and they ask them what happened, the pupil's immediate response is, 'The teacher hates me!' Right or wrong, pupils are offering a genuine, heartfelt interpretation. They may have been punished for behaving irresponsibly. They believe, however, that the teacher is 'playing the man and not the ball' and has sent them out because he or she has something against them personally. Whether it is rewarding or punishing, teachers have to constantly clarify that they are responding to the behaviour, not playing favourites or getting even.

Recognising responsible behaviour

When defining responsible or fair behaviour it is essential to be very specific so there is no confusion about its acceptability. For example, it is not enough to decide that the pupils should stop being 'irresponsible' when what you really want is the pupils to bring all necessary equipment to class and be prepared to try set work. Increased clarity on your part allows you to transmit a clearer request to pupils, which should result in a greater likelihood of conformity by the children. The amount of clarity required will be largely determined by the age of the pupils. A young pupil may need to be told to 'Put your reader back in the desk, take out your Maths book and turn to the page you are up to'. An older child may be able to cope with a more general instruction like 'Get ready for Maths'.

> Whether it is rewarding or punishing, teachers have to constantly clarify that they are responding to the behaviour, not playing favourites or getting even.

Once the behavioural indicators of responsibility are defined, it is necessary to decide the amount of flexibility you can cope with before risking becoming inconsistent. For example, do you want pupils to take turns in answering without calling out, *all* the time, or only when you are 'at the front'? What if the calling out is a genuine attempt at the right answer? Once you have determined the behavioural goals, the next step is deciding what consequences will apply when the goals are achieved or not achieved.

When pupils act responsibly

One might assume that teachers are so appreciative of pupils' efforts that they would automatically give recognition. As discussed in Chapter 2, however, secondary teachers only sometimes recognise pupils' appropriate behaviour. It appears that they take pupils' socially responsible behaviour for granted without realising that, by occasionally demonstrating approval, it can be strengthened.

Everybody feels good when his or her efforts are recognised. Pupils base their opinions about themselves, their self-concepts, on the way in which others, including teachers, respond to their behaviour. For example, they may decide whether they are good or bad, kind or cruel, nice or nasty, liked or even likeable. They are particularly likely to be positively influenced by a teacher's descriptive praise or reward. In addition, they will feel good about their relationship with their teacher.

Five types of approving responses can be identified:

1. very specific verbal praise, such as, 'John, I appreciated the way you shared your calculator with Amera today', or 'Thank you for helping your classmate'
2. non-verbal praise such as a smile, wink or nod
3. communication to others such as good notes, stickers or phone calls to parents
4. the provision of special privileges, like free time, access to the computer, or being a monitor
5. material rewards like sweets or stationery.

Each of these can be offered to individual pupils or the class as a whole.

To determine the most effective rewards, you can ask your pupils questions like:

What would you like to do more often at school?

Where would you like to go more often?

Who would you like to spend more time working with?

If you had £2 to spend at school, what would you buy?

These and other more detailed questions can help to identify the most effective rewards for each pupil. It is important that the reward be appropriate and varied. In this context, it is useful to note that verbal praise in classrooms is a little tricky. Research indicates that at levels above Grade 4, pupils may be embarrassed by public praise, although private praise, or praise communicated privately to parents or other teachers, is acceptable (Lewis, Lovegrove and Burman 1991).

It is critical that teachers recognise responsible behaviour, whether or not it results in achievement. Some recent research (Crawford and Beaman, 2007) presents an interesting analysis of teachers' use of recognitions. She reports on surveys of 145 teachers, and direct observations of 79, to conclude that when it comes to pupils' academically appropriate behaviour, teachers are quick to offer recognition. In contrast, however, teachers don't see a need to say thank you, or offer any other sort of recognition, when pupils act in a socially appropriate manner.

It seems that showing respect for the rights of classmates to learn, and to feel emotionally and physically safe, is assumed to be an obligation and therefore not worthy of note. However, if teachers only reward work produced, pupils who require motivation to behave responsibly (those in Categories B, C and D) may remain outside the reward system and some may even try to destroy it. Ironically, those pupils most likely to receive recognition (Category A) may be prevented from developing their own intrinsic motivation and become more dependent rather than independent learners.

Despite the theoretical requirement of individualised rewards, I have found it extremely time-consuming providing even the same rewards for all pupils. The tangible rewards I settled on when teaching included a variety of letters to parents such as: 'I am pleased to inform you that (pupil's name) tried very hard/cooperated well/was very helpful … in class today.' I was fascinated to note that even some boys in Year 10 were prepared to collect such a letter, as long as they were able to do so privately.

Other, tangible rewards were required in my Year 7 class, and these were introduced as part of a points system, whereby I recognised the individual pupil's responsible behaviour by allotting him or her a point. Once they had accumulated 20 points, which normally took two to three weeks, pupils received a prize. Since I controlled the allotment of points, and marked them into a folder, I was able to make sure that the more challenging pupils didn't fall behind. Because I was not a 'natural' at recognising responsible behaviour, or even that comfortable in giving rewards for being 'normal', I required a system. I based it around what are called 'transitions', the moments in a lesson when I requested that pupils change activities.

I was aware that work done by Kounin (1970) identified transitions as the times when pupils were most likely to misbehave. During transitions, I walked to my desk and picked up a folder containing a class list. It was coloured bright yellow to ensure that pupils noticed. Whenever there was a transition in the lesson from one kind of activity to another, I looked for pupils who were ready to begin the next activity, said something like 'Enzo's ready', and gave the pupil a point. Even a Category D pupil can get ready. For prizes, the pupils were able to select from a collection of stationery, football cards, and some lollies. Although I found it impossible to individualise rewards, I frequently asked pupils what they would like me to put into the collection of goodies. I must admit that I even offered sherbet to one particular, hyperactive pupil … then ushered him to his next class.

During a trip to America in 1995, I located a number of inner suburban schools that used rewards as a way of dealing with very difficult pupils. One of the most committed was a school in Pennsylvania, which was concerned about absenteeism. Staff had gone to insurance companies in the local community, who were happy to help keep kids off the streets, out of other people's homes, and in school. Consequently, they contributed approximately $10 000 a term, which the school spent on a second-hand car. This vehicle became the prize in a raffle, tickets in which were issued to pupils based on their attendance records and responsible behaviour in the classroom and the schoolyard. An evaluation of this strategy reports that during the year in which attendance earned raffle tickets, absenteeism dropped substantially.

In addition to implementing classroom-based recognitions of responsible behaviour, teachers can also involve parents. The most effective rewards may be those provided by parents as a prearranged response to a note from the teacher. For example, if a pupil obtains a note praising his or her cooperation or effort, parents may allow a little more TV, pocket money or some other privilege.

It is important to emphasise the effect of an assertive non-verbal response. When you give pupils an approving message, you should approach them physically, lean forward, smile, and look them in the eye to increase the effect of your message. For example, noticing Sarah helping another pupil, Igor, you might look her squarely in the eye, smile, lean forward, and say something like, 'The way you helped Igor was a pleasure to watch, keep it up!' Alternatively, you might look at Sarah and say, 'Well done, that's a point to you!' or 'That's a class point!' It needs to be understood that a fixed number of points leads to an individual or class privilege, such as access to the computer or free time.

> When you give pupils an approving message, you should approach them physically, lean forward, smile, and look them in the eye to increase the effect of your message.

Because many teachers, especially secondary school teachers, are unlikely to use recognitions and rewards frequently (Lewis, 2006; Lewis *et al.*, 1991) it may be necessary to become *very* systematic.

One teacher I worked with decided to recognise good behaviour in his Year 7 class by periodically assessing the proportion of the class that was on task at randomly selected moments throughout the lesson, and awarding class points accordingly: 100 per cent on task = ten points, 80 per cent = eight points, 30 per cent = three points, and so on. To assist himself, he played a 60-minute tape containing ten randomly placed beeps that acted as his signal to take a reading of the class's on-task behaviour. Class points, when cashed in, provided free time for the class as a whole. He found the system very effective and ensured pupils had some ongoing recognition for their good behaviour.

Three final issues need to be emphasised when it comes to rewards and recognitions:

1. *Reward effort, not behaviour.* The first is that teachers should frequently explain that rewards are not for responsible behaviour per se, which all pupils have an obligation

> Reward effort, not behaviour.

to perform. Such behaviour is designed to protect rights and is expected of pupils because it is fair and reasonable. It is not optional. What needs to be emphasised is that it is the *effort* required to behave responsibly that is being recognised. Obviously, for Category A pupils, who fully appreciate the rights of their classmates, know what's right, and are accustomed to acting in a socially appropriate way, the effort is minimal.

In contrast, for Category C and D pupils sometimes the effort can be enormous. When recognising effort, teachers should occasionally say something like: 'We appreciate the effort you've made. I know it's not always easy to do the right thing.' This way, pupils will not develop the idea that they are only behaving in a particular way to receive a reward. Rather, they will see themselves as doing what is right because it is right, while at the same time understanding that their efforts are being appreciated. It also prepares the ground for teachers to confront the well-behaved pupils if they complain about a challenging pupil getting recognition often, even though he rarely acts appropriately. This brings us to the second issue, minimising rewards as soon as possible.

> Rewards and recognitions need to be kept to a minimum.

2. *Rewards and recognitions need to be kept to a minimum*. In order to minimise the use of rewards and recognitions it will be necessary to convince pupils to give them up. The following dialogue indicates what may need to be said to a Category A pupil who has come to complain that she needs more rewards and recognitions.

> Hi Cleo, I'm glad you chose to speak with me. I think you're correct about Serge getting more recognition for acting responsibly than you do. The thing is, it's not that I think he's better than you or anything like that, it's just that I think that some kids aren't yet as mature or responsible as others. These kids therefore have to make more effort if they are to behave reasonably and protect people's rights. It's the effort kids make that I'm recognising, not the behaviour. Everybody is obliged to respect rights. I feel Serge needs the recognition I give him, because I think it takes him a fair bit of effort. If you are less mature than I thought you were, and you don't really appreciate the idea of rights, tell me what I need to offer you as a bribe for you to be reasonable enough to act fairly.

I have had conversations like this, usually with girls whom I would have thought were in Category A. They generally accepted the situation and were quite pleased to end the conversation. If necessary, I also made more of an effort to catch them being 'good'. In their case, that related more to displays of Communal responsibility. Furthermore, the form of recognition was mainly verbal, rather than tangible.

In addition to trying to prevent escalation of rewards and recognition with individual pupils, it is possible to minimise the nature of rewards at a class level. When working with my Year 7, using the points system described above, I was able to address the class after about four months and say:

> Some of you are growing up. You no longer need to be bribed to do the right thing. You know what it means to act responsibly and protect rights. I will continue to give you points but if you don't cash in for prizes, it just means you don't need to be bribed to do what you already know is correct.

After my speech to that class, approximately 50 per cent stopped cashing in. I deliberately continued giving them points for appropriate behaviour so I could say how impressive it was when they got to 60 or more points without cashing in. Among other things, it saved me a fortune.

Teachers need to get pupils to do the right thing because it is the right thing, not only because it gets recognised by others. Eventually, if pupils learn that certain behaviours are responsible and, because they require effort, that effort will be recognised, it should be possible for teachers to use the non-interventional techniques outlined in the previous chapter, and have pupils self-regulate their behaviour. They should not require outside manipulation. However, if hints and rewards don't work, then it will be necessary to employ Coercive power.

3. *Reward Communal responsibility more heavily than Personal responsibility.* The third issue of significance has to do with the amount of recognition offered for the two types of responsibility discussed in Chapter 3 (Personal and Communal). Recent research (Lewis, 2001) shows that pupils are generally more willing to do the right thing than they are to encourage their classmates to act responsibly.

> Pupils are generally more willing to do the right thing than they are to encourage their classmates to act responsibly.

Even the majority of the most responsible pupils in Israeli and Australian classrooms are unlikely to encourage their classmates to be reasonable (Romi *et al.*, 2008). This is particularly the case in secondary schools.

Primary (Year 6) pupils see themselves as quite responsible. They describe themselves as likely to protect rights in the classroom, but less likely to encourage others to do likewise. A secondary pupil's level of responsibility is significantly lower, with regard to their willingness to protect rights, and to encourage classmates to act responsibly. It is, on average, 'mostly' like them to do the former and only 'a little' like them to do the latter (Lewis, 2001).

Consequently, we should provide greater incentive for pupils (particularly those in secondary schools) to encourage their classmates to do the right thing. For example, if a pupil is ready and waiting at the beginning of a lesson, it need not be acknowledged, or alternatively, one point might be earned. However, if that pupil, at the beginning of the lesson, reminds a classmate that 'we are waiting to begin', then it should definitely be acknowledged with a 'thanks', or two points (rather than one) might be earned. Similarly, a pupil listening while others are answering a question may not draw recognition or reward, whereas reminding a classmate to be quiet so others can hear will be recognised.

When pupils act irresponsibly

When a pupil, unaffected by hints and recognition of appropriate behaviour, displays a lack of concern for the rights of other pupils, negative consequences should follow, to convince him or her to act more responsibly. It is essential that pupils know in advance the consequences the teacher will use. This will reduce the likelihood of resistance due to perceived unfairness.

When you are choosing which consequences to use, it is advisable to select a consequence that seems to fit the 'crime'. Your pupils can more readily see that the consequence experienced is a result of their own action. In this way, although you are giving the child an unpleasant experience, there is a smaller drain on the pile of goodwill. Some examples of 'logical' consequences are: talking excessively to a friend and preventing others from hearing means being seated separately; failing to bring necessary books means doing the work at home; intentionally breaking another pupil's ruler means buying a replacement. Nevertheless, negative consequences are still things that pupils should prefer not to have happen.

There are six kinds of negative consequences commonly used in schools. The first two of these involve separation of the pupil from his or her friends. The first occurs in the classroom, whereas the second involves placing the pupil somewhere other than in the classroom. This usually means in some other teacher's class or some designated spot in the school, such as in the office of a senior staff member. Separation also comes in two forms, 'time-out' and detention. The difference between these two depends on who decides when the pupil returns to the class.

In contrast to detention, during which uncompleted work is finished, extra work is attempted, lines are written, discussion about the behaviour problem occurs, or the pupil is asked to simply sit and be bored, 'time-out' is not to be seen as a punishment. Time-out isolation should occur in a place where the pupil is comfortable and not 'in disgrace'. The main objective for a pupil who gets time-out is to plan for a better future. Specifically, the pupil is required to write out a plan for his or her future behaviour that should preclude the possibility of the inappropriate behaviour happening again.

Time-out must be seen as a response to inappropriate behaviour that leaves the pupil with the choice of whether or not to behave. Therefore, pupils must not be put in time-out for a set period, as this would be tantamount to a detention. Rather, pupils must stay there only until they are prepared to work out the problem. To assist them, many schools provide a series of questions pupils are asked to address.

The following set of questions is used by one secondary school for which I have provided professional development:

- What did you do that caused you to be in time-out?
- Why did you do it?
- Was it responsible?
- What were likely to be some good outcomes of what you did?
- What were likely to be some bad outcomes of what you did?
- What could you do instead if the same situation were to recur?
- What do you plan to do instead? What is more responsible?

Once a decision has been made to act responsibly in the future, the pupil is free to return and try afresh.

Because time-out is not a punishment, teachers must be careful about the language they use when sending pupils there. For example, it would be inappropriate to say what I once witnessed a teacher say:

> You! Get to time-out! Now!

It should sound more like:

> You know that you can only stay in class if you are willing to be fair. Please go to the time-out room. See if you can figure out how to handle a situation like this better next time. As soon as you've got it worked out, come and speak to me. Hopefully, it won't take too long.

Likewise, the teacher should greet the returning pupil pleasantly, but be very concrete about the pupil's plan. For example:

> It's good to see you were able to sort this out. You say here that you will act better. What exactly do you mean? What do you plan to do if … ?

One of the more extreme examples of misuse of isolation with pupils was shown to me in a school in Texas in 1995. The school, like a number of others in America, has an ISS (In School Suspension) room. On entering it, I noted the supervising teacher's desk and filing cabinet and then the corrals for pupils. The room contained 16 stalls. Each had walls approximately 180 cm high and a door 150 cm high. There was a desk/shelf and chair in each cubicle. All the cubicles had been painted with a matt black paint. So were all the walls.

In this school, pupils on ISS entered their cubicle at the beginning of the school day and left at the day's end. At 10.30 a.m. and 2.30 p.m., a uniformed guard and a very heavily built teacher, over 180 cm tall, would escort pupils to and from the toilets. These were the only times pupils left their cubicles. Lunches had to be eaten at the desks. The supervising teacher was responsible for passing work from classroom teachers to the pupils in their cubicles, returning completed work and shaking awake any pupils who attempted to sleep. Pupils in this school could be placed in ISS for up to three days for offences ranging from repetitive tardiness or failure to submit homework, to physical assault.

A third type of consequence involves removal of privileges such as free time, excursions, practical work, and so on. A fourth involves sending the pupil to another teacher, for example a senior teacher, year-level coordinator or assistant principal. A fifth relates to informing the parents, who can provide a prearranged punishment for their child when notified of the pupil's behaviour in school. A sixth and possibly ultimate consequence could be temporary suspension from school.

When dealing with Category B pupils, it is justifiable to use the same hierarchy of consequences regardless of the offence. The first response, however, should be an explanation. This highlights the way that inappropriate behaviour interferes with the rights of others. Thereafter, any pupil who fails to correct his or her behaviour is ignoring the legitimate rights of his or her classmates and defying the legitimate authority of the teacher, who, as explained in the previous chapter, has been empowered by the class to deal with pupils who ignore rights. Pupils who continue with irresponsible behaviour can then be treated in the same way regardless of whether the initial offence was rocking on a chair, calling out, moving around the room or swearing at a fellow pupil.

As mentioned earlier, when giving praise your body language should be consistent with your spoken message. You should have a similar awareness of your body language when telling pupils about the consequences you are going to apply. This time it is advisable to look serious, move towards pupils, lean towards them, and look into their eyes. Although some teacher-oriented approaches talk of holding a pupil's arm, in most states in Australia this may be construed as assault, and hence should be avoided.

Informing the pupils

As explained above, expectations for appropriate pupil behaviour need to be based on the rights of pupils to learn as much as possible and to be free from harassment. All consequences need to be established at the beginning of the school year, preferably at a classroom meeting. The time to set expectations and to inform pupils of the positive and negative consequences of their behaviour is when both the pupils and the teacher are calm and there is the time and opportunity to talk without interruption.

After this meeting, the class expectations, the rewards and recognitions to be provided to responsible pupils, and the consequences for not acting responsibly, should be written down and put somewhere obvious. They should also be acknowledged by the parents of each pupil. It is probably wise to work out a set of increasingly punitive consequences so that pupils will know what happens the first time they act irresponsibly, the second time, and so on. In Figure 5.1 (page 62) is a pro-forma that I supply to teachers who are preparing their classroom management plan. Within the plan, there is no attempt to describe all responsible (and by implication irresponsible) behaviour. There is instead an assumption that you can evaluate behaviour by relating it to the two rights stated on the plan.

In 1995, I was invited to assist a large secondary school develop an approach to discipline and pupil welfare. As a first step, I surveyed the preferences of 23 members of the school council, all 104 teachers, and a 10 per cent (representative) sample of pupils and parents for the range of consequences to be used by teachers in the school.

Negative consequences most suitable for use within the secondary school were argued to be those supported (as 'definitely' or 'probably' suitable) by two-thirds or more of the members of the school council, two-thirds or more of parents and at least 60 per cent of pupils, and if at least two-thirds or more of teachers who were using the technique reported that it was working well for them.

In total the negative consequences supported by the school community and perceived by staff as effective were:

- verbally correcting pupils' behaviour
- rearranging seating of 1) individual pupils or 2) the class
- having a discussion with a pupil after class
- sending a pupil out of class for a short 'cooling off' period
- giving yard-cleaning duty to individual pupils
- giving lunchtime detentions to individual pupils
- seeking help regarding individual pupils from 1) level coordinators or 2) home room teachers
- writing a letter to parents of individual pupils

(continued on page 63)

Classroom Rights And Responsibilities

In this classroom:

1. Pupils and the teacher have the right to do as much work as possible.

Therefore:
- pupils should bring (encourage others to bring) all their equipment to class
- pupils should listen (encourage others to listen) when pupils are speaking
- pupils should be (encourage others to be) on time
- pupils should attempt (encourage others to attempt) all work.

2. Pupils and the teacher have the right to feel comfortable and safe in the classroom.

Therefore:
- pupils should pass (encourage others to pass) all objects hand to hand
- pupils should speak (encourage others to speak) to others politely
- pupils should keep (encourage others to keep) their hands to themselves.

If pupils make the effort to respect the rights of others, their effort will be recognised by giving them:	If pupils don't make the effort to respect the rights of others, the following will occur (in order):

Pupil's signature: ....

Parent's signature: ....

Understanding Pupil Behaviour Copyright © Lewis 2009

Figure 5.1   Pro-forma management plan

- having a discussion with parents of pupils
- making pupils pay restitution for property damage.

Consideration of these negative consequences shows that they bear a close relationship to the findings of published research on the most acceptable punishments (Lewis, 2005). It would be easy to arrange a number of these, hierarchically, into an assertive management plan.

Responding to inappropriate behaviour

When you need to tell pupils that their behaviour is interfering with the rights of other pupils, four stages are recommended:

1. identify the pupil
2. describe the behaviour
3. indicate which rights are being denied
4. demand responsible behaviour.

The order in which these stages are communicated is very important. The reason is that, although most Category B pupils feel that their teachers like them, the same may not be true for pupils in Categories C and D.

Consequently, were a teacher to ask Category C or D pupils to 'please be quiet!', it is possible they will feel he or she doesn't like them and is acting unfairly. They may actually feel that the teacher has said 'I don't like you, therefore be quiet'. Even if a teacher says 'You're talking, please be quiet' they may still feel that he or she said 'You're talking, I don't like you, please be quiet'.

Unless teachers make clear the assumption underlying their intervention (i.e., that some behaviour is unfair because it infringes the rights of classmates), some pupils may assume something less user-friendly. Finally, when explaining, it is important to put the message into short bursts of words, as the more difficult the pupil is, the less likely he or she is to be able to process more than five words in a row due to limited listening skills (Rowe and Rowe, 2006).

In the box below (page 64) are listed a number of ways of explaining various misdemeanours.

When delivering these explanations, you need to choose the level of non-verbal language to accompany the explanation. For example, to keep the intervention low-key you may choose to address the irresponsible behaviour some time after it occurred by waiting until the class is engaged in seatwork. Then you could quietly crouch next to, and a little below, the 'target' pupil before quietly explaining what the problem was. In this way, there is minimal non-verbal provocation (almost essential when dealing with C and D pupils).

Talking when teacher is trying to talk to class:

David, you're talking. These kids can't hear. Please be quiet (Please act responsibly/Please be fair).

Calling out:

David, you're calling out. Others have a right to concentrate. Please be quiet.

Not having equipment:

David, you need your equipment to learn. When you borrow from others it distracts them. Please bring all your things to class.

Putting down other students:

David, Cleo has a right to feel comfortable. You are not respecting her rights. Please speak nicely.

When you speak disrespectfully to Cleo, David, she feels bad. She has a right to feel safe. Be careful how you say things.

Coming late to class:

David, when you come late to class you aren't being fair. It distracts others. Please come on time.

Fighting:

Fighting puts people at risk of being hurt. Everyone has a right to feel safe. Please keep your hands to yourself.

Eating in class:

David, when you eat, others are distracted. Please don't eat in class.

In contrast, you may wish to address the irresponsible behaviour from across the classroom. If so, there should be unambiguously strong non-verbal cues: you should face towards the child, look him or her in the eye and lean forward as you speak. Body language is very important for the more difficult pupils, because, as discussed later in this book, although they may be less literate, C and D pupils are more visually capable than most pupils.

In many cases such a verbal demand will stimulate a pupil response such as, 'But it's not my fault because ...' Such reactions by pupils should not sidetrack you, no matter what. When confronted by an excuse or an explanation, or even a provocative tone, you must remember that this is not the time to address it, and that you first need to deal with the irresponsible behaviour. Sometimes pupils will try to sidetrack and control the teacher by using an insolent tone, raised voice, rolling of the eyes or exasperated sigh.

In the face of any provocative response or verbal resistance to the initial demand, move into the second stage and *calmly repeat your demand*. For example, say 'I understand' or 'I hear you' and then repeat your original demand. This 'broken record' routine or reassertion is essential to show that your immediate aim is to stop the inappropriate behaviour. The routine can be used a number of times if necessary. It is important to note that at no time should you sound angry. The repetition of the demand must be done calmly.

There are two very important reasons for calmness. The first is because we now have evidence that the way children's brains develop means that even when they are acting like adults they are not using their brains in the same way as adults (Luna and Sweeney, 2004; Spear, 2000; Strauch, 2003). Brain scans demonstrate that the brain continues to develop until the age of about 25 (Giedd, 2004). Therefore, an adolescent's brain is a work in progress. As a result, they frequently respond more emotionally or intuitively than an adult does, with less regard for any natural or logical consequences that are sure to follow. This is particularly likely to happen when they are under stress. According to Beatriz Luna, when things are running smoothly, they can act like adults. However, if they are stressed, all that can break down. Yelling at a Category B pupil, or even sounding a bit officious to a Category C or D pupil, may stress them to the point that they cease to operate rationally.

> Brain scans demonstrate that the brain continues to develop until the age of about 25 ... As a result, they frequently respond more emotionally or intuitively than an adult does, with less regard for any natural or logical consequences that are sure to follow.

The second reason to ensure you remain calm is the need to provide an appropriate model for children. Once you become aggressive, in any form, your belief in the rights of the pupil to be free from harassment is under question. According to Gary Fenstermacher, the best way to create responsible pupils is to ensure that they are around responsible teachers: 'The manner of a teacher takes on particular importance, insofar as it serves as a model for the pupils ... as something the pupil will see and believe proper, or imitate, or accept as a standard for how things will be' (2001, p. 644).

In conclusion, as argued by Robert Roeser, Jacquelynne Eccles and Arnold Sameroff (2000, p. 454), 'Teachers need to protect adolescents from situations they perceive as threatening to their self … or threatening to their social image.' If not, then 'adolescents will feel less motivated to learn and more unhappy and will be more likely to manifest academic or social problems'. Consequently, teachers must remain calm so that both they and the pupil will not become locked into a destructive cycle.

If calm repetitions don't work – and often they won't – then you move into the third stage, which is to offer the offending pupil a choice. The choice is straightforward: either stop the unacceptable behaviour or accept an unpleasant and undesired consequence. For example, you might say, 'Georgia, you have a choice, either you sit squarely on the chair or you will stand at the back for five minutes.' The choice is largely a matter of illusion because the aim is not really to offer a choice but to stop the inappropriate behaviour, hence the need for an increasingly punitive hierarchy of consequences.

Therefore, in stage 3, when addressing a talker, you might say something like, 'Look, Con, you have a choice. Either you stop talking to Janet or you will be seated elsewhere.' However, the choice is not a real one, because if the first consequence fails to stop the talking and it recurs after Con has been moved, you now say, 'Con, if you choose to talk, you will be moved totally on your own and have 15 minutes' detention to catch up on the work you miss.' In other words, you up the ante until the pupil gives in. Given the premise that pupils must learn to respect rights, you have to do whatever is necessary to make pupils behave responsibly.

Nevertheless, if pupils resist to the point that they say they will not follow your instructions (e.g. to change seats), you should not argue. It is better to hear the resistance and calm the pupil by acknowledging the reality of the situation. This will sound something like:

> James, I don't intend to force you. However, if you choose not to move, then immediately after this lesson finishes I am *going* to … The choice is yours. You have ten seconds to think about it.

At this point, you go about your business and see what happens.

The following dialogue illustrates the sequence of events:

> *T:* (calm/not hostile – open stance, leaning forward, eye contact, waiting one second after saying the pupil's name to ensure there is eye contact and three seconds after warning to allow for the expected compliance) James … your talk is disturbing others. They have a right to work. Please be quiet.

J: But I'm talking about the work. I can't do my work if I don't talk.

T: I understand but you must be quiet.

James continues talking a few seconds later.

T: James, you have a choice … you either stop talking or sit over there where you won't bother anyone.

James is quiet for a minute or two but then continues talking.

T: Please sit over there, James.

J: No, I won't. There is no way you can make me!

T: James, you're right. I can't make you. However, if you don't move, you will have to go to Mr Mathews's room and we will talk at lunchtime.'

J: I don't care!

T: James, please leave now. I'll see you at lunchtime. Stephen [a classmate], please accompany James to Mr Mathews's office.

If the pupil's motive, excuse or explanation for the inappropriate behaviour is so important that it needs to be discussed, he or she will resist accordingly, and you will move through the series of consequences until you reach one that removes the pupil from the classroom, or even requires someone to come and collect the pupil. Any pupil who gets this far becomes a Category C pupil. To summarise how to behave with Category B pupils, Figure 5.2 (page 68) outlines a plan that I have successfully implemented in a number of very difficult primary and secondary grades.

A final comment on negative consequences relates to the earlier discussion highlighting the need to provide stronger recognition for Communal responsibility than for Personal responsibility. We need to explain to our pupils that, just as it is a very commendable act to encourage others to behave responsibly, it is very inappropriate to encourage others to behave irresponsibly, particularly when a teacher is trying to do the opposite.

Consequently, any pupil who butts in when you are trying to manage the inappropriate behaviour of a classmate should receive quite severe consequences. Most teachers know the problem. They are in the midst of addressing a pupil about his or her inappropriate behaviour when another pupil joins in, on the side of the miscreant. Since it becomes impossible to speak to two pupils at once, you are at a considerable disadvantage. One way of dealing with this is to explain to the class, in a calm moment, that if a pupil attempts to butt in, there will be a non-verbal signal from you which means 'please stay out of this, it is very irresponsible to encourage others to do the wrong thing'.

Principles

Base all actions on the learning and safety needs of other pupils.
Act against the misbehaviour but show (and state) liking for the child.
Let the child realise that antisocial behaviour results in a risk of isolation from 'friends'. Remain calm.

Step 1
Make the expectations for appropriate behaviour very clear.
Base expectations on the need for pupils to feel emotionally and physically safe and to learn as much as possible.

Step 2
Set up classroom as shown — with three or four seats or desks on the door side of the room. Don't be worried about jamming up the seats in the 'working' block.

Door   Outside seats   Working block seats

Step 3
When appropriate behaviour occurs provide recognition.
Provide some form of recognition for appropriate behaviour (*particularly for pupils who are being punished*). Encourage difficult children.
Create a 'Transition' recognition folder. Make it a bright colour. Every time you change the nature of the activity (e.g. 'Open your books', 'Move into groups', that is, 'transitions') ignore those who are slow and give ticks to those who move faster. Say 'X is ready', 'Y has her book open', etc. After 20 ticks, give a reward.

Step 4
When inappropriate behaviour occurs apply six sequential steps:
1. Provide explanation.
2. Reassert.
3. Move pupil to another seat in the 'working block' of seats.
4. Move pupil to one of the 'outside' seats until they feel they are ready to return and act responsibly.
5. Move pupil to outside seat for remainder of lesson.
6. Send pupil out and now treat the child as a Category C student.

Figure 5.2   Setting up a system for classroom discipline

For example, the signal could be an outstretched arm with the palm pointing forwards. Any further pupil intervention and you point to the back of the room, which means 'Move to the back, I'll discuss this butting in later'. Any further involvement by the pupil, and you point to the door, which means 'Please wait outside, we will discuss this later'. This non-verbal system allows you, more or less, to maintain verbal contact with the original target pupil and to 'overlap', that is, do two things at once (Kounin, 1970).

Before moving on to discussing pupils who do not respond to recognitions or punishments by becoming more responsible, I wish to make two observations about using a systematic, stepped consequence system. Because I generally like to maximise the freedom of pupils, I initially use two explanations, followed by moving the pupil to another part of the class, followed by five minutes' isolation, then 15 minutes' isolation, then detention, and so on. This protracted sequence of sanctions gives pupils many opportunities to exercise self-control and to learn to act more responsibly.

I find, however, that there are occasions when the gradual increase in the severity of sanctions is a major disadvantage. When running a discussion or conducting a demonstration, when I want pupils to listen carefully and contribute efficiently to the discussion, I find that too much time can be lost in explanations and requests to move, and the momentum of the lesson can be severely affected. At such times, therefore, I adopt a modified system for such 'full frontal' teaching. During this time I notify pupils that there will be two explanations, then a detention. As long as the pupils are fully aware of any switch in the sequence of sanctions, I find they accept the change and adapt to the more severe sequence by becoming less likely to call out or otherwise run foul of the class expectations for appropriate behaviour.

The second difficulty also relates to the inflexibility associated with a systematic stepped series of consequences. Often I have found myself separating and moving pupils for what were very minor infractions, and resenting the fact that I seemed to have no choice but to move to the next level of sanction when the behaviour recurred. Initially, I attempted to overcome this problem by selective use of multiple reassertions, thereby avoiding the more severe level of sanction. However, because it was selective, pupils rightly claimed that I gave some pupils more leeway than others.

Ultimately, I found a way to deal with my frustration, gaining greater flexibility of response while still maintaining the security of a system and avoiding the legitimate criticism of my pupils. During times when the pupils are not dependent on my directions, for example during small-group work or individual seatwork, I use explanations and reassertions but do not graduate to more severe sanctions. Only when, and if, I feel it is necessary to take firmer control, due to an increase in the frequency or significance of the disruption, do I formally advise the class that we are moving into our six-step system. I am then able to systematically maintain a hierarchy of sanctions like separation, isolation, detention, and contacting parents, until it feels right to relax my hold and quietly revert to explanations and reassertion. In this way, I can slip in and out of the system at will, thereby gaining greater flexibility in my response to inappropriate pupil behaviour.

You may need to consider using a number of systems, each with a different set of punishments, rewards and recognitions. Then at particular stages of a lesson, or during particular lessons, it would be possible to indicate to pupils which approach you are implementing. The approach described here allows for considerable flexibility. The core of it is that in responding to the needs of Category B pupils, teachers should develop at least one set of both positive (encouraging) and negative (discouraging) consequences to follow responsible and irresponsible behaviours respectively, inform pupils of the respective consequences, and not allow any reactions by a pupil to prevent them from calmly and assertively acting to protect pupils' rights. Under no circumstances should they allow pupils to control them.

If pupils fail to respond to hints, rewards and punishments, they are no longer considered as belonging to Category B, but need to be viewed as Category C pupils. The way teachers should work with such pupils is to talk with them, as shown in the next chapter, so that they can be helped to act more responsibly.

6 | Responding to pupils manifesting Category C behaviour

As indicated in Chapters 4 and 5, some pupils won't respect their classmates' learning and safety rights, regardless of teacher hints, explanations, recognitions and rewards, or punishments. These pupils will ultimately be asked to leave the room. This will be done in a calm way and only after they have either repeatedly acted irresponsibly or have overtly refused to cooperate.

Another rare possibility is that they have acted in a way that is very damaging to themselves, to others, or to equipment. In such a case, there may be no explanation or intermediate steps. For example, one can hardly imagine a situation where one pupil is hitting another with a machete and the teacher says: 'Michael, you are hitting Teo and putting his blood all over the floor. He may get seriously hurt. Also, someone could slip on the blood. Please put down the hatchet.' The reason for the removal of a pupil is not retribution for the inappropriateness of his or her behaviour. Exiting a pupil is simply an admission that this pupil is currently unable or unwilling to act in the best interests of his or her classmates.

If this were to happen occasionally, it does not mean that the pupil needs to be considered as a Category C. It may simply be a question of increasing your pile of goodwill with the pupil by showing more interest in him or her as an individual. It may be that you are forgetting to catch the pupil acting responsibly, and taking advantage of the opportunity to say something nice. It may mean that you need to reconsider the kinds of rewards or consequences you are using with that particular pupil. You may even have to engage in an unnatural act and be nice to a Neanderthal when he's acting 'normal'. If, however, despite your attempts to keep the pupil in the room (and in Category B), he or she has to leave the room twice in a week, or four times in a month, then it is essential that the teacher and pupil have a talk, the nature of which I will outline below.

Category C pupils

It is interesting to reflect on what currently occurs in many schools I visit. When pupils repeatedly act irresponsibly or overtly refuse to cooperate they are asked (often ordered) to leave the room. Sometimes teachers are able to do this respectfully and sometimes not. Voices are raised, fingers are pointed, doors are slammed. The pupil is frequently told to report to a senior teacher, such as a deputy principal or year coordinator. These are usually very experienced teachers. They know that it is not very useful to pull rank with these pupils, especially when they are already excited.

So, rather than lay on Legitimate and Coercive power, which they correctly surmise will not work well on this pupil at this time, they attempt to have a conversation with the pupil which sometimes sounds like the following:

T: Ah Megan, not again. What happened this time?

M: She hates me!

T: Come on, Megan, your teacher doesn't hate you. All she's trying to do is teach your friends what they've come here to learn, and keep them feeling safe while they're doing it. I reckon you're a good kid. I know how well you are doing in Drama and Music, for example. Do you think you can stay out of trouble for the rest of the day if I send you back? I tell you what. If you can stay out of trouble for the rest of today and tomorrow, and don't let me down, come and see me at the end of tomorrow and I'll give you a bag of chips. Do you agree? Can you just go back and be normal?

M: Yeah.

T: OK. Now go back and stay out of trouble.

Clearly, this experienced senior teacher has done what the research discussed in Chapters 1 and 2 would recommend: use Reward and Referent power. It is also what nearly all the teachers participating in my professional development programmes say is most likely to work with more challenging pupils. Nevertheless, when the pupil returns to class the dialogue often sounds like this:

T: Megan, what are you doing back here? I sent you to Mr Black.

M: Yeah. He spoke to me and said to come back and to be normal.

T: What else did Mr Black do? Was there a detention?

M: No! No! He didn't punish me. He said he'd give me a bag of chips!

At this point, the teacher usually thinks or says something like 'Bloody administration. They never support you in this school.'

To ensure that the Referent power of teachers is maximised, it is essential that any pupil who is asked to leave class often enough to be considered a Category C pupil speaks only with the teacher who asked him or her to leave. In some schools with which I consult, the senior teacher will 'mind', but not talk with, the pupil. In others, the teacher sets seatwork and the senior teacher will come and look after the class while the teacher talks with the exited pupil. In yet others, the pupil is sent to the back of the room of a cooperating teacher. This could be a private or school-wide arrangement.

In one school I've worked with, teachers who exit pupils send them to the school's reception area. When they arrive, a secretary checks a list of available classes and sends the pupil to sit in the back of a class where the pupils are at least two years older or younger than the exited pupil. The Assistant Principal developed a form which indicates only the time pupils are exited from the classroom, the time they arrive at reception, the time they arrive at the other class and what work they are expected to do. The Assistant Principal said he deliberately left off any reference to what pupil misbehaviour led to the exit as it's entirely between the teacher and the pupil. It's nobody else's business.

Of course, if exited pupils misbehave in the new class they are then sent to a senior teacher; otherwise they are ignored. It really doesn't matter where a pupil is sent, as long as he or she is ignored, and as long as the pupil is not sent to a place where other exited pupils have been sent. In each case, the pupil is free to work or to contemplate what went wrong and what needs now to be done. Some schools provide a worksheet, which includes questions like those detailed in Chapter 3, to facilitate such reflection (a detailed example of such a worksheet is given in Figure 9.3).

The pupil should gain nothing by being exited. If it becomes a badge of courage to join other exited pupils (often Category D pupils), then there is something to be gained by being sent out. Three incidents, which occurred in separate secondary schools, illustrate the problem.

In one, 13 pupils from four Year 9 classes arranged one day to meet in the school's time-out room at a predetermined time. The second incident was reported in the following words by an observer participating in a research study on classroom processes:

> A student entered the classroom ten minutes late. He was not reprimanded by the teacher. He slammed down his books but the teacher ignored the noise. Five minutes later, the student raised his hand. Student requested

to go to the time-out room. The teacher was a little stunned (and so was I). Recovering quickly, the teacher asked the student whether there was a particular reason for such a request. The student then replied, 'I'm meeting my girlfriend there at 2 p.m. and I've got two minutes to get there in time. If I don't it will be the end of us!'

The third happened when I was visiting a large private school. As I was waiting to observe a teacher and about to knock and enter the room, a pupil was exited. We both stood in an extremely long corridor. As he came out, I noticed that he semaphored to mates who had been exited from their respective classes. I was clearly in the happening place. This was hardly isolation.

These three incidents indicate that some pupils view the time-out room as a social outlet rather than as a non-punitive space for self-evaluation and analysis.

Talking with pupils displaying Category C behaviour

Pupils characterised by Category C behaviour can be distinguished from Category D pupils in that the former, when calm, are aware of their motives, are sensitive to the legitimate rights of others, are able to identify with the feelings of others and have concern for others. Consequently a Category C pupil would be happy to modify any behaviour that was adversely impacting on the legitimate rights of others, unless he or she felt the behaviour was absolutely necessary.

> The main idea of talking with pupils is to re-establish their commitment to rights and to acknowledge the inappropriateness of the behaviour that led to the exiting.

The main idea of talking with pupils is to re-establish their commitment to rights and to acknowledge the inappropriateness of the behaviour that led to the exiting. To understand the aim of 'the talk' more easily, it is helpful to consider Eric Berne's *Theory of Transactional Analysis* (1961, 1964). According to his analysis, each of us has three elements or 'states'. These are the 'Parent', 'Child', and 'Adult' states. In brief, they can be described as follows:

The *Parent* is the part of us that has been conditioned by the authority figures in our upbringing. It comprises a huge number of demands, sanctions, embargos and restrictions.

The *Child* is the emotional and feeling part of us. When in one's Child it is not necessary to be logical or feel responsible.

The *Adult* is our rational, responsible, moral and logical part. When in an adult state we are reasonable and assertive, processing data objectively and dealing fairly with the information we are taking in. Our adult is our ability to think and determine action for ourselves, based on received data. The adult in us is the 'grown-up' rational person who talks reasonably and assertively, neither trying to control nor reacting.

In summary, the parent state is the hub of values, the adult state is the hub of logic and rationality, and the child state is the hub of emotions.

The aim of the talk is to keep the Category C pupil in his or her adult state. This is because someone in an adult state is open to logic, remorse and conviction, all of which are crucial elements of the talking process. So it is not a good idea to conduct the talk when the pupil is in class or even in visual contact with other pupils. If you do, they have two audiences: you, an adult, and their peers, children. In such a contest the pupil's child state often wins.

Pupils find it very uncomfortable to be confronted in the adult state because it is extremely difficult to lie when in an adult state, and it is hard not to respond to reason. To be irresponsible requires a shift of state. This, by the way, is why many pupils will address teachers very provocatively during a discussion that is focusing on their irresponsible behaviour. It usually occurs when the pupil is feeling under pressure. Rather than suffer the discomfort associated with feeling remorse or guilt, it is a very attractive (and probably unconscious) option to say something that will push the teacher into his or her parent state. If successful, the pupil can then adopt the natural partner to this, the child state.

A recent example illustrates such dialogue:

T: Are you saying that it's OK for you to distract your friends when they're trying to concentrate?

S: Well, you're a shit teacher!

Without realising it, the pupil wants the teacher to say something like 'Don't speak to me like that'. Such a statement comes from the parent state. It would then allow the pupil to be 'off the hook' because the natural response to a teacher in an apparent parent state is to remain in a child state, with no feelings of remorse or responsibility.

A second example I heard recently occurred when a male pupil, during a one-on-one discussion with a teacher, was feeling pressured to bring his equipment to class and to stop bothering his mates who were trying to work. He suddenly leant forward, looked the female teacher squarely in the eye and said. 'What's the matter with you at the moment, miss? You seem a bit uptight. Is it that time of month?'

For children (or anyone else for that matter) to remain in an adult state they must feel 'heard' and understood. Consequently, the 'talk' involves a lot of listening. One of the best-known systems that can be used to exemplify the style of the talk is Teacher Effectiveness Training (TET), devised by Gordon (1975). This process uses a great deal of active listening to assist in the clarification of problems, hopefully leading to some resolution. Although the following is based on such a style there are, as will be shown, significant differences.

In brief, the aim of talking with Category C pupils is to calm them, give them the opportunity to talk through their side of the story, and provide them with information to confront any irrational ideas they may have regarding the appropriateness of their behaviour. This is done so that they can clearly identify that there was a problem with the way they behaved in class. When this is successful, the aim is to have them propose alternative ways of behaving, help them evaluate the alternatives, and implement the one they think is best for them. It is also important to have them agree to a review period after which the solution is evaluated.

In total there are nine steps in a productive discussion:

1. Welcome.
2. Seek the pupil's help to deal with the 'problem'.
3. State what the problem is and what effect it is having on others (including you) and how it makes you feel.
4. Listen, and paraphrase the pupil's facts and feelings. Reframe what is heard, to reassure the pupil.
5. Confront the irrational parts of the pupil's argument. Try to show that he or she is unreasonable.
6. Get the pupil's agreement that there is a 'problem'.
7. Have the pupil provide a solution that meets both his or her and your needs; if necessary, suggest some solutions.
8. Clearly define the selected solution.
9. Set a timetable to evaluate its effectiveness.

Step 1 Welcome.

Often when pupils are spoken with, or rather, spoken to, by teachers, the latter take on the air of a parent. The welcome, therefore, may sound like 'Come in, Alexis. Sit down'. To attempt to get the pupil into his adult state the welcome should be adult to adult. For example, 'Glad you made it, Alexis, good to see you'.

Step 2 Seek the pupil's help to deal with the problem.

To allow the pupil to feel more on the same level as the teacher in the conversation, he or she is asked to assist the teacher, who expresses a need for assistance. For example, 'I need you to help me understand what happened in class', or 'There's something I hope you can help me with'.

Step 3 State what the problem is, what effect it is having on others (including you) and how it makes you feel.

Most pupils are sent out of classes for one of three reasons. First, they may have repeated a minor misbehaviour such as moving or talking when they were not meant to, rocking on their chairs, or handling an irrelevant distracting object (e.g. a mobile phone), despite the teacher's repeated demands that they stop. Alternatively, they may have argued with the teacher when the latter tried to stop them misbehaving. Finally, they may have done something seriously inappropriate, like use racist or sexist language, or engage in physical violence. The aim of the teacher when talking with Category C pupils is to engage their adult, to allow them ownership of both the problem and the solution. Therefore, rather than telling them that their behaviour is unacceptable, you share your concern about its negative impact on others by stating an I-message.

In an I-message three things are identified, which may be presented in any order:

- the pupil behaviour that is causing a problem for classmates, the teacher or both
- the tangible or concrete effect the pupil's behaviour has on classmates, the teacher or both
- how the teacher feels as a result of the behaviour.

I-messages let pupils know that their behaviour is creating a problem without blaming them for anything or telling them what to do. They can be contrasted with messages that place the responsibility for the teacher's problem directly on the pupil ('you are making me angry', 'you are behaving stupidly', 'you are never finished on time', or 'you must stop that immediately'). In the 'talk' with Category C pupils, the I-message is modified to focus primarily on the problem the pupil's behaviour is causing his or her classmates.

Some examples will illustrate. Suppose that you had to exit a pupil for repeatedly talking at the wrong times. Having greeted and empowered the pupil, you might say something like, 'When you talk at the same time as I am talking to the class, your mates can't hear, and I feel concerned.' The same message can be delivered by putting the three parts in a different order, for example, 'I get concerned when pupils' attempts to hear me are interrupted by your talking.'

Some further examples of I-messages useful to an average classroom teacher might be:

I feel worried when you come late because it distracts the rest of the pupils and they need to concentrate on the beginning of the lesson. They will lose out.

I'm concerned that someone will be hurt if pupils fight.

It distracts pupils when you come late to class, and I get frustrated.

I get annoyed when you consistently call out answers too quickly because other pupils don't get a fair go.

When you throw things like staplers in the classroom, I get worried that some of your friends may get hurt.

It is assumed that one of the prime reasons for Category C pupils' problem behaviour is that they don't realise the effect their behaviour has on others because they are too engrossed in achieving their own goals. However, once made aware of their classmates' (and your) problem, they may be ready to engage in solving it by modifying their behaviour. In response to I-messages from you, Category C pupils will be considerate enough to modify their behaviour, or at least to enter into discussion as to why they believe their behaviour is really appropriate.

A desire by pupils to 'look after' their classmates assumes that they have a genuine commitment to the two rights possessed by all pupils: the right to an opportunity to learn and the right to feel physically and emotionally safe.

Such a desire by pupils to 'look after' their classmates assumes that they have a genuine commitment to the two rights possessed by all pupils: the right to an opportunity to learn and the right to feel physically and emotionally safe. Their desire to look after you as well assumes that you have estabished the pile of goodwill referred to earlier. Without this goodwill, and without trust in your motives, pupils may not respond positively, even when they become aware of the plight of their fellow pupils, and yourself. In other words, if you haven't developed a relationship with a pupil to the point that the child cares about your welfare, I-messages (or anything else for that matter) may not work.

Given that you have succeeded in establishing a reasonable relationship with the Category C pupil, an I-message should prompt the child to negotiate a change in behaviour. However, there will be occasions when the behaviour that you judge to be inappropriate is seen by the pupil as behaviour that he or she 'needs' to engage in. A typical example could be when a child persistently seeks help from a friend while you are talking to the class. When this is the case, an I-message from you is likely to result in a verbal response from the pupil, defending or explaining the behaviour. It is at this point that you move to Step 4, that is, active listening.

Step 4 Listen, and paraphrase the pupil's facts and feelings, then reframe what is heard to reassure the pupil.

To listen actively teachers need to repeat what the pupil told them, using other words to show that they have processed the information. They should also try to work out how the pupil is feeling and reflect that as well. Fortunately, pupils who are exited and need to be treated as Category C pupils tend to say the same sort of things to teachers:

It wasn't me.

There were others.

I was only talking about the work.

I threw it because she needed it in a hurry.

She started it.

I can't come on time, my mum brings me.

I lost my books so I can't bring them.

Listening can be done at differing depths. You can simply restate the pupil's words in your own, look for the unspoken underlying message or even notice the underlying feelings that you believe are built into the message. For example, assume a pupil said 'It wasn't me'. The process of listening at increasing levels of depth is illustrated below.

- *It wasn't me.* 'So there were others talking also?' (restating words).
- *It wasn't me.* 'Do you think I'm singling you out unfairly?' (highlighting the underlying message).
- *It wasn't me.* 'Are you upset because you think I'm picking on you?' (strengthening the underlying message).
- *It wasn't me.* 'Are you angry because you think I don't like you?' (identifying implicit feelings).

Listening while validating

If possible, when listening, it is easier to keep pupils in an adult state if you can clearly separate your rejection of the behaviour from your understanding that the pupil is generally a nice person. For example, if a pupil who is in trouble for swearing at a classmate says he made me', you could say, 'so you wouldn't normally swear at other pupils, you only swore at him because you were provoked'. This process is called a reframe and presents the pupil in a positive light while allowing him or her to own the behaviour.

The following examples further illustrate the technique:

- *I was only talking about the work.* 'So if you knew what was going on you wouldn't have interrupted anybody?'
- *I threw it because she needed it in a hurry.* 'If it wasn't so urgent you wouldn't have thrown it? You were only trying to help?'
- *I lost my books so I can't bring them.* 'So the only reason you're not bringing your stuff is because it's lost?'

This technique allows pupils a way of accepting that they did the 'wrong' thing without feeling that you see them as a bad person. By using this technique, you can protect your pile of goodwill while confronting the pupil's inappropriate behaviour. The joy of the technique is that if pupils accept your proposition, they are implicitly acknowledging ownership of their inappropriate behaviour. This of course allows you to follow up with 'So, you did speak (interrupt/swear/throw)'.

When involved in listening to pupils, you need to refrain from asking for additional information, contradicting, offering advice, or negating the pupil's feeling. Often you will find listening without inputting information quite difficult. Nevertheless, listening well is a great way to keep pupils in their adult state. All the way through the process of the 'talk', it is important to listen whenever the pupil says something new, or even if he or she repeats the same information.

In the course of listening, you may need to be prepared to hear the same statement several times. This is often because at crucial times in the conversation the pupil may seek reassurance that they are still acceptable, even if they have behaved inappropriately. This can sometimes be irritating, but pupils wouldn't say something if they didn't want it heard.

Teachers must be prepared to listen not only to verbal communication from pupils but also to non-verbal messages. For example, a pupil may appear for a 'talk' but sit side on to the teacher, facing away with arms folded. If the teacher says the traditional 'Please look at me', he or she has adopted a parent state. This permits pupils to remain in the child state and accept no responsibility for their behaviour. Rather, the teacher must listen to the body language and say something like, 'I can see you are unhappy to be here. Do you feel I'm being unfair in asking to talk with you?' Such listening will usually prompt a verbal response which then begins the 'talk'. Once listened to, many verbal responses or excuses offered by pupils for their inappropriate behaviour will need to be confronted, because they are irrational.

Step 5 Confront the irrational parts of the pupil's argument. Try to show they are unreasonable.

The confrontation stage of the talk usually follows the listening stage, although, as stated above, listening occurs in response to any pupil contribution to the conversation. In general, the confrontation involves stating what is unreasonable about the pupil's behaviour or excuses. The joy of confronting pupils' irrational thinking is that in many cases it's very predictable.

As indicated above, to justify their behaviour C pupils say things like:

There were others.

I was only talking about the work.

I threw it because she needed it in a hurry.

She started it.

I can't come on time, my mum brings me.

I lost my books so I can't bring them.

Consider the first of these. So what if there were others. Even if other pupils are acting irresponsibly, it doesn't justify an adult doing likewise. It is not a rational excuse. When a pupil is in an adult state, you can successfully confront him/her by asking, 'Are you saying that because other pupils aren't prepared to respect the rights of their classmates, that justifies you interfering with your friends' learning?' To deflect some other issues associated with pupils feeling singled out, you could say, 'Look, I don't think you would like it if I spoke about you with others so I don't think it's fair to talk about others here. You agree that you were talking?'

Although it is not possible to identify 'the' confrontation for every possible excuse, the following exemplify the idea. Note that most invite a response by being in the form of a question.

- *I was only talking about the work.* 'But are you saying that your need to keep up justifies interfering with the learning of your friends?'
- *I threw it because she needed it in a hurry.* 'So you feel it's OK to place your friends in danger to save a few seconds?'

→

- *She started it.* 'Are you saying that because she did the wrong thing that justifies you handling it so unreasonably?'
- *I can't come on time, my mum brings me.* 'So there's nothing you can do to get here on time? Nothing at all?'
- *I lost my books so I can't bring them.* 'So because you haven't made the effort to replace the lost stuff, you feel it's OK to keep interfering with your classmates' learning by borrowing their stuff?'

The idea is to give pupils additional information that can't be assimilated if they continue to hang on to their irrational excuse. This causes stress to the adult because of the energy required to hold to two contradictory positions.

Confrontation via a hypothetical

A second standard form of confrontation takes the form of asking the pupil to think about a hypothetical situation to show how irrational his or her excuse is. One of my favourites is what was said in response to a tough kid who was trying to justify his aggressive behaviour. In defence, he said to his teacher: 'Look! School is like that. Some kids are a bit rough with others. Everyone expects it. It's no big deal.' First, the teacher listened: 'So really a bit of rough stuff among pupils is OK. Teachers should butt out.' The pupil said 'Yeah'.

The teacher confronted the response by presenting the following hypothetical situation: 'OK then, if tomorrow we take into your grade a kid who's 190 cm and 90 kg, tougher than you, and doesn't like the way you look, are you saying we shouldn't get involved if he wants to rearrange your face?' The example is a little extreme but it makes the point.

Developing challenging confrontations is not easy. Nevertheless, it is not hard either, particularly when it's done by a group of teachers. Practice makes perfect, and after all, the excuses you will hear don't vary that much from year to year, decade to decade. Nevertheless, there will be times when a pupil will give you an excuse that you aren't able to easily confront: 'But my Dad says hit first, don't throw the second punch.' If such a situation should occur, simply say to the pupil: 'Hmm, OK, I need to think about what you've said. I'm going to mull it over tonight and catch up with you tomorrow.' Then it's time to ring a friend or two to work out a challenging confrontation with which you feel comfortable.

Confrontation via repeated questioning

Asking a pupil the same question a number of times can be a very powerful confrontational device when the pupil is in an adult state and attempts to lie. As stated above, it is very difficult for a person to lie knowingly when in the adult state. A pupil has to invest a lot of energy in repeatedly lying, in the face of what he or she knows to be a reasonable, calm and adult confrontation.

A pupil might find it difficult to sustain the following dialogue:

T: Hi Alexis, glad you could make it. I need you to help me. Today in class I asked you repeatedly not to interrupt your friends. They were trying to get the work done. When I asked you to stop you denied everything and argued, which was even more distracting. That's not really fair to them.

A: I didn't say anything in class!

T: Nothing?

A: Not a thing!

T: There was no time today that you talked at the wrong time?

A: No!

T: No time at all?

A: Not really.

T: Not once?

It may well be at this stage that a pupil will say something like 'I wasn't the only one'. This then gives you an opportunity to listen: 'So you weren't the only one who interfered with other kids' learning.' Any agreement, of course, indicates the pupil's tacit acknowledgment that he or she was talking at the wrong time.

Step 6 Get the pupil's agreement that there is a 'problem'.

In general, after welcoming, seeking help, stating what you perceive to be the problem, then listening and confronting, you should eventually get to a situation where it will be possible to have the pupil recognise that his or her behaviour is problematic. Usually this is done by saying, 'So you can see that there is a problem.' Don't settle for maybe.

The following illustrates a typical dialogue:

T: Hi Alexis, good to see you. I'm hoping you can help me understand something. Today in class when I tried to stop you interrupting the learning of your friends you argued with me. What was that all about?

A: I was only talking about the work. You made such a fuss.

T: So you feel I overreacted because all you wanted to do was your own work?

A: Yeah.

T: But you seem to be suggesting that it's OK if your need to keep up overrides some other pupils' right to learn.

A: I didn't say that. But all I did was talk about the work.

T: So you weren't trying to distract anybody, you just wanted to get on with your work. Do you think I overreacted?

A: Yeah.

T: The only reason I said anything was because I could see that your friends were being distracted.

A: What am I supposed to do then?

T: OK. You seem to recognise that it's not fair for you to distract your mates even if all you're doing is talking about the work.

A: Maybe.

T: You're not sure? Can't you see it's unfair?

A: Yeah, I suppose.

T: You still don't sound sure. Are you sure?

A: Yeah.

At this point the dialogue moves to Step 7.

Step 7 Have the pupil provide a solution that meets both his or her and your needs; if necessary, suggest some solutions.

There are various ways of finding a solution that is acceptable to both parties. You can start a discussion by saying something like, 'Let's try to work out some ways we can solve this problem.' Alternatively, you and the pupil can independently write down all the ways in which the problem could be resolved to both your satisfaction, and then eliminate any that either of you finds totally unacceptable. In general terms what you are requesting is that the pupil tells you what he or she plans to do if the same situation that stimulated the problematic behaviour were to recur.

It is very important for you to be honest in stating your feelings, and if you feel that a proposed solution is unfair to other pupils or to you, you must say so. In order to achieve a solution jointly with the pupil, consider all the solutions that remain after the elimination step, and together decide which of the remaining is best. While occasionally a mutually acceptable solution might not be found, in general one exists and finding it simply requires more negotiation. The following example, taken from my teaching, will clarify the idea.

Jim was a pupil who had a tendency to answer back. Whenever I judged his behaviour to be inappropriate and told him so, he seemed compelled to argue that I was wrong and that he was not to blame. In discussion, I explained to Jim that our interactions at these times used up a lot of class time and distracted a lot of kids. Once he was ready to recognise that his behaviour was a problem, I asked him how he could solve this problem: 'If I became aware in class that your talking was disturbing your classmates and I asked you to stop, how would you handle it in a way that your friends' right to learn was not ignored?'

The three options Jim put forward to solve this problem were:

1. I should watch more closely and not blame him unfairly.
2. I shouldn't argue with him but rather accept his opinion.
3. He should let it pass even if he thought I was wrong.

Further discussion quickly showed that options 1 and 2 were unacceptable to me and option 3 was not feasible for Jim to carry out. Even though ideally he should provide the solution to be implemented, I could see that it was going to take too long, so I suggested that rather than argue with me at the time, Jim could see me at lunchtime to present his side of the story. Jim thought this was too great an imposition on his time. He was unhappy with that and consequently a little more motivated to find a different, workable solution. Ultimately, Jim and I agreed that we would try a system whereby he would write down his side of the story at the time of having his behaviour corrected, and I would reply, either in writing that night or verbally the next day.

Within a couple of lessons, Jim was in trouble for talking when he shouldn't have been, and began to argue about my interpretation of his behaviour ('I wasn't talking, I was just movin' my lips'). When I reminded him of our agreement, twice, he stopped arguing, but didn't write a note. The next lesson he was asked to stop grabbing at Erica's pencil case and begrudgingly did so. This time he immediately proceeded to write a note of complaint, which he handed to me as he left class. In it, Jim explained that Erica had thrown his book off the desk and he was just retaliating. I answered in writing that I could only respond to behaviour I saw, and being human, I couldn't see everything. Nevertheless, I was obliged to respond to behaviour I saw or chaos would ensue. I also said that I would keep a close eye on Erica. After this, Jim generally stopped answering back and did not write any more notes, although on a number of occasions he complained verbally after class.

Successful completion of this solution-finding step in the pupil-oriented approach requires you to use your intelligence and imagination to develop possible solutions. Although you may find it very difficult to be sufficiently creative to start with, teachers generally improve with practice.

Step 8 Clearly define the selected solution.

As a result of agreeing on a solution to a problem, it is often necessary to decide something like 'who is to do what and when? What do we need, and who will get it?' For example, using the solution Jim and I agreed upon, it was necessary to make sure that Jim had pieces of paper on which he was to write his side of the story. The story had to be to the point and completed within five minutes. I had to reply within 24 hours.

Step 9 Set a timetable to evaluate its effectiveness.

The final element in the discussion is checking that the solution agreed upon is seen to work to the satisfaction of both pupil and teacher. Often some fine-tuning to remove remaining wrinkles is required after the solution is implemented, although there will be some occasions when one or both parties are unhappy with a solution that looked all right to them initially. This involves saying something like, 'OK we'll try that for a week. Let's meet very briefly on Friday after class to see that it's all working as it should.'

Goodwill and the talk

By concentrating on understanding the Category C pupils' view of problems that arise in classrooms, your responses will communicate your regard for them. By treating pupils almost as equals, you will maintain a high-quality teacher–pupil relationship and consequently a large pile of goodwill. Your refusal to pull rank, and thereby devalue their feelings and perceptions, will ensure that you have sufficient goodwill to enable pupils to compromise when it comes to identifying a workable solution to a problem.

> By treating pupils almost as equals, you will maintain a high-quality teacher–pupil relationship and consequently a large pile of goodwill.

If, however, after three or four talks, you see no improvement in the pupil's behaviour in class, then you have probably been talking to a Category D pupil. Further, when you try to draw on the Referent power in class by saying something like 'Come on, Josh, you said you were going to handle it differently', and you sense no remorse, then it's time to consider the possibility that this Category C pupil is really a Category D. Another way you might tell is if the pupil ever, in reference to his classmates, says, 'they're not my friends', or 'they don't like me', and sounds as if he really means it. Any pupil who says this and means it is probably a Category D pupil. Chapter 7 will address their needs.

7 | Responding to pupils manifesting Category D behaviour

As indicated in Chapters 4, 5 and 6, pupils displaying Category D behaviour patterns don't respond to hints, rewards and recognitions, demands, punishment and one-on-one adult-to-adult talks. These are the pupils you have tried everything with, to no avail. Sometimes there is a little improvement here and there, but there is no real sense that the pupil is becoming more responsible and more aware of the rights of others.

In contrast to Category C pupils, there is little benefit in conducting one-on-one discussions with Category D pupils. The reason for this is that it is extremely difficult to tap into their adult state, and they can't discuss their motivation because they don't have a conscious awareness of it.

Category D pupils are typically grouped into four different subcategories, as will be explained later. In reality, a Category D pupil will often show behaviours characteristic of two of the four subcategories, less frequently, three of them. The way to think about the behaviour of pupils in this category is not in terms of how severe or minor the misbehaviour, but rather how repetitive it is.

Even speaking of pupils as Category D is misleading because a pupil may act as a Category A pupil in one setting and a Category D pupil in another, as will be discussed later in this chapter. It is even possible for a pupil to operate as a Category D for a part of a lesson – for example, whenever the reading of complex text is required – and Category A during the role-play.

Basic assumptions

Unlike previous chapters, this chapter relies entirely on one theory, the group-oriented approach developed by Dreikurs. The key assumptions we will apply to Category D pupils are applied to all pupils by Dreikurs. In the Developmental Management Approach outlined in this book, however, only Category D pupils will be considered in Dreikurs' terms.

Underlying Dreikurs' approach is an assumption that all children want to belong, that is, they want status and recognition, and all of their behaviour is based on their desire to be accepted into a group. Furthermore, all their inappropriate behaviour reflects mistaken beliefs that through this type of behaviour they will gain the recognition they need. A second assumption is that they will curb their

> All children want to belong, that is, they want status and recognition, and all of their behaviour is based on their desire to belong to a group.

inappropriate behaviour only if they believe this will result in their gaining acceptance by a group that is important to them.

One of the most interesting, but usually unstated, implications of these assumptions is the tremendously important role of the pile of goodwill. When teachers don't make enough effort to develop and maintain a pile of goodwill with a particular pupil, then that pupil may turn to inappropriate behaviour as a way of gaining recognition.

Inappropriate behaviour

The most significant contribution of the Dreikurs approach is its explanation of why Category D pupils behave inappropriately.

The best way to explain the inappropriate behaviour of pupils designated as Categories A, B or C is to assume that the pupils need to relieve a temporary emotional state such as frustration, anxiety, boredom, fear or excitement. Their behaviour is a response to some part of their environment. For example, sometimes pupils misbehave because they are confused or bored by the type of instruction they are receiving (McInerney and McInerney, 2002), or by the way the teacher handles their misbehaviour (Lewis, 2006). Sometimes it is because they have some very important information, unrelated to the aims the teacher had in mind for the lesson, which needs to be shared – *now*!

Their behaviour may also be caused by things that are going on around them at the time; for example, Con 'explodes' and hits Jackie because she takes a ruler away from him. Their misbehaviour is very context-dependent and they have a clear understanding of what they are doing. Pupils in Category A and B also know that what they do is wrong, when it is wrong. In contrast, as explained in Chapter 6, pupils in Category C may need more time and direction to explore their moral compass before acknowledging the inappropriateness of their misbehaviour.

Pupils in Category D are very different. They do not understand why they act inappropriately. In fact, one of the things teachers need to do to help such pupils is to make sure someone puts them in touch with their (hypothetical) motive, to see if they can recognise it. Perhaps the best way to describe Category D pupils' reasons for acting inappropriately is to describe their behaviour as somehow meeting unarticulated needs. That is, they act in a socially inappropriate way to satisfy personal needs.

Pupils whose behaviour fits this category tend to repeatedly disrupt regardless of variations in the teachers' treatment. Their behaviour is due to their attempts to be significant, to gain recognition. They believe, albeit wrongly, that their misbehaviour will result in them gaining the recognition they want. They always *choose* to engage in whatever behaviour they display, although they are generally not conscious of their motive. The argument rests on a belief that pupils demonstrating Category D behaviour would prefer to choose to act in an acceptable manner to obtain recognition, but they believe it is not possible to achieve such recognition through normal channels.

The reason for a pupil making the choice to act inappropriately has to do with feelings of discouragement. By an early stage of life, some children become very discouraged. They come to believe that they are not much good at making a go of most things. They see people around them as much better than they are at getting on in the world through normal channels. True or not, some children see it this way, and once they latch on to the idea that they aren't as capable as others, they tend to see everything in distorted ways so that their beliefs about themselves are supported.

For example, a pupil who feels her older brother is much smarter than she could see her teacher's genuine interest in her achievements as motivated by some sort of sympathy for her relative incompetence. Her perception of her teacher's behaviour is distorted by her bad feelings about herself.

As a result of the feeling that it's not worth competing for recognition in socially acceptable ways, discouraged children will give up trying to be acceptable. Their lack of confidence in their abilities can be contrasted with the self-evaluation of Category A, B and C pupils who, because they are confident of their ability to find a place within a social group and to belong through constructive activity, will tend not to be an ongoing problem. These individuals have developed feelings of equality and self-worth. They are interested in cooperating with others, and in participating usefully within a group. They face nearly all school demands, be they intellectual, social, physical, or emotional, with confidence in their ability to cope. There is no need for them to misbehave because they know they can function constructively and cooperatively in the class.

Not all discouraged pupils, however, are failures at what they do. Some are aware of their competencies and believe that teachers (and parents) like them, but only as long as they do well in their schoolwork. Often these children may be the first-born in their families. They feel that their worth depends on what they can achieve, not on who they are, and although they generally perform at above average, or even a high level, it is never good enough. The problem is that even though they look as if they have a right to be satisfied with themselves, they aren't. Feeling that they can never do well enough to be worthwhile, these pupils can also adopt a different goal from that of being acceptable.

Sources of discouragement in the family

In any family, it is likely that unacceptable behaviour occurs as part of the normal pattern of life. Situations arise within all families that result in children feeling rejected. The structure of the family system inevitably means that subsystems or subgroups develop: the parent or parents, in theory, form a subgroup with certain goals that may make it essential to override the needs of other subgroups within the family. For example, parents have a need for privacy if they are to maintain a sexual relationship. This means that parents have to establish rules within their families to guard these needs. The pursuit of these parental rights may cause conflict and resentment, and even feelings of rejection among the children. In large families, the adolescent children may form subgroups of their own and be the group most affected by parents' attempts to guard their privacy.

> It is important for teachers to be aware that pupils pick up most of these feelings of rejection at home, even if the patterns are not apparent to outsiders. It can also happen very early in the life of the child.

Another issue within families that can generate feelings of discouragement in children is the hierarchical position of family members relative to each other. This structure imposes restrictions on family members' free choice of roles. Position within a family is largely determined socially (parents have certain duties to perform) and biologically (adolescents require more autonomy than 6-year-olds). For example, older children may resent a younger sibling staying up late where they regard this as their unique right. They may feel discouraged by what they see as a lack of recognition for their position in the family, and these feelings can be played out in the classroom.

Imagine a situation where an older child in a family is expected to help look after the baby, clean the table, and sweep the floor. He may feel resentful and fight with the 5-year-old, who is mainly free of responsibilities, and consequently is seen to be more favoured. In another family, the younger children may vigorously complain of rejection when forced to go to bed earlier than their older brothers or sisters.

Sibling rivalry can be caused, and prevented, by the way in which parents balance these differing rights or responsibilities. In the case of sibling rivalry, not only can the feelings of discouragement be transferred to the classroom, but the patterns of the family interactions themselves can be manifested between pupils. For example, if a child is very resentful of an older sibling's need to be 'correct' all the time, he or she may react with hostility towards a classmate with similar tendencies. Teachers are then in a position to exacerbate or ameliorate these patterns of behaviour.

One pattern of discouragement very commonly referred to appears to surround second-born children. It has been argued (e.g. Leman, 1985; Isaacson and Radish, 2002) that first-born children are strivers and, generally, achievers. They tend to read, write and do 'rithmetic quite well, as that is how they gain recognition from their parents. The second-born may feel he or she cannot compete and will frequently skill up in areas not dominated by the first-borns. This is often within areas of music, sport, or art – second-borns are often very creative. A less positive outcome for second-borns is that they reject the norms of the family and can slip into patterns of misbehaviour.

These birth-order patterns are not immutable. It is the pattern of interactions within families, which result in a child feeling rejected or not, that we must consider. When children feel inadequate, the result can be chronically unacceptable behaviour, which becomes part of the fabric and challenge that make up the classroom. It is therefore important for us to be aware of the child's need, so we can avoid adding to the rejection felt by Category D pupils who are behaving inappropriately. This is easy to say, but hard to deliver. Category D pupils are experts at controlling the responses of teachers and parents.

> When children feel inadequate, the result can be chronically unacceptable behaviour, which becomes part of the fabric and challenge that make up the classroom.

I can recall an example from when I was teaching in a relatively tough school. One day, while on lunch duty, I noticed two boys arguing. One was much bigger than the other. By the time I was able to approach them, the larger boy had picked up the smaller one by the neck and had him pressed against a wire fence. Although the boy was not choking, he was clearly uncomfortable and unhappy. When I told the larger boy to put the other boy down, he looked me over with disdain and said: 'Why don't you butt out?' Looking him in the eye, I said exactly the wrong thing: 'What sort of an animal are you?'

This sort of comment was not going to reduce the pupil's sense of rejection. I was effectively controlled by the pupil. He was clearly an expert in manipulating the reaction of those around him. Most Category D pupils are.

Aims of inappropriate behaviour

To help identify the Category D pupils, all you have to do is think of the pupils you would consider to be the most difficult to teach. Then you focus on the behaviour these children manifest. Once you start to see the patterns forming you will discover that there are four main types. That is because there are four main aims of children's inappropriate behaviour. Because the real aim of all children is to be liked and appreciated, these four aims are called *mistaken goals*. Dreikurs identifies these aims as:

1. *attention-seeking:* the need to get special attention
2. *power-seeking:* the need to get other people to do what they (the pupils) want, or to show that they won't do what others want
3. *revenge-seeking:* the need to hurt others as much as they feel hurt by others
4. *withdrawal:* the need to be left alone.

These four goals are all likely to arise in the average classroom. In my experience, it is only in a small proportion of cases that the behaviour is so severe that the classroom is no longer able to fulfil its basic functions, that of teaching and learning. When a pupil's motive to behave inappropriately strongly outweighs his or her choice for so-called normal behaviour, the pupil may become extremely difficult to handle and can create an acute problem requiring extra help.

For instance, if a large amount of the pupil's time is spent in withdrawal, vandalising school property or displaying aggressive defiance, then he or she is not carrying out other developmental functions. The situation would then be described as an acute or pathological one, requiring the assistance of a qualified counsellor. The inappropriate behaviour of Category D pupils, however, generally assumes less dramatic forms. Often it is attention-seeking, comprising low-level behaviour like talking, making noises, rocking on chairs, and/or moving inappropriately. The reason it is a problem is that, although it stops when the teacher addresses the inappropriate behaviour, it recurs and seems to keep recurring over and over again.

Although it is common for a difficult pupil to be operating under one of the four mistaken goals at any particular time, some pupils do move from goal to goal. Dreikurs argues that pupils initially misbehave due to a desire for attention, and it is only if they conclude that they are not gaining sufficient recognition through this way of behaving that they move on to behaviour arising from their need for power, revenge or withdrawal. If, however, they believe they are gaining enough recognition, and hence satisfaction, from attention-seeking, power or revenge, they will continue behaving in accordance with the corresponding mistaken goal until they are helped to see the situation they are in and the choices they have made.

Since an understanding of a pupil's mistaken goals is so integral to Dreikurs' group-oriented approach, I will give a more detailed description of the behavioural characteristics of each. In general, for each of the four mistaken goals, the way you feel when exposed to a given pupil's behaviour is your best guide to which goal they have selected as the basis for their behaviour.

1. Attention-seeking

If the goal of a pupil's behaviour is attention-seeking, you usually feel irritated or annoyed. But your feelings do not offer an infallible guide. You may be very likely to react with irritation if you have just come from an exhausting staff meeting and a pupil persists in his or her legitimate request for a piece of equipment needed for a class experiment. Unless a pupil's behaviour is regularly annoying, the problem may simply be a result of the pupil's insensitivity.

As indicated above, with attention-seeking behaviour, the behaviour usually stops after being attended to, but only for a short time, and then it recurs with monotonous regularity. A pupil's attention-seeking behaviour is essentially aimed at tying up the attention of the teacher. It can range from disruptive or boisterous behaviour to habitual forgetfulness.

Balson (1992) identifies typical examples of attention-seeking behaviour, among which are children whom he calls the 'walking question mark', the 'clown', the 'sloppy or slow worker', and the 'bashful or shy' child. Added to this list are 'the persistent talker', the 'noise maker', the 'wanderer', and the 'child who never follows directions unless prompted'.

Not all attention-seeking takes on a destructive form. Some attention-seekers will be compelled to produce excellent work. The only problem is that their teacher *has* to recognise it, regardless of whether there are 25 other pupils awaiting instructions at the time. Such pupils are likely to act in a range of ways designed to attract positive feedback from their teacher.

In summary, the characteristic pattern for an attention-seeker is that the child behaves inappropriately, the teacher responds, the child stops acting inappropriately for a short time, then does the same or some other inappropriate behaviour once more, and the cycle repeats itself.

2. Power-seeking

A pupil whose mistaken goal is the need to make people do as he or she says, or the need not to do as others say, usually make teachers consistently feel confronted, angry and retaliatory. These pupils' view of the world is that they are recognised as worthwhile only as long as they are in charge and the boss. If people don't let them do as they please, it's because people don't approve of them. Pupils who have power as their mistaken goal are often argumentative, deceitful, contradictory, tantrum-prone or stubborn.

Unlike attention-seekers, pupils who are into power rarely respond to a normal telling-off by temporarily stopping their behaviour. They usually resist in some way and try to draw their teacher into a fight. Although classic power-seekers are the arguers, the provocateurs and the resisters, in its more helpful forms a need for power may be expressed as a need for control and leadership. Consequently, such power-seeking pupils can make great 'helpers'. They are often excellent at getting things done, like distributing books or preparing the props for a school play.

3. Revenge-seeking

The third of the four mistaken goals is a belief, held by some children, that they can only feel important when they can hurt other people as much as they feel others have and will hurt them. They consistently make teachers feel threatened, hurt or frightened. Such pupils behave in very hurtful ways: they steal, destroy property, or are violent and vicious. They are so discouraged that the only way they can regain some sense of status is to get even, to hit back at their 'persecutors'.

They consider evidence of other people's dislike of them as some sort of positive achievement. If and when their hurtful behaviour provokes others to hurt them back, they feel even more justified in seeking revenge. Their main aim is to hurt. Sometimes it's to hurt others, sometimes themselves (e.g. self-mutilation) and sometimes it is things (property) that they attempt to damage.

4. Withdrawal

The last resort of pupils who are very deeply discouraged is withdrawal. Rather than respond to the perceived injustices dealt to them by others, withdrawing pupils give up. Their only aim is to avoid further rejection by appearing so stupid or by being so unavailable that they hope they will be left alone. Teachers who have to deal with withdrawing pupils generally feel powerless and tend to despair.

The withdrawal need not be thought of as covering all fields of endeavour. Usually it is only in areas where the pupils feel their inadequacies most acutely that the misbehaviour is most frequent. Nevertheless, some D pupils convey the impression that they cannot manage to do anything correctly. By and large, most 'incompetent' pupils have the ability to achieve. They are just profoundly discouraged. Because such pupils see themselves as failures, they no longer have any reason to try. They hope that if they are left alone, their perceived incompetence will be overlooked, and they will no longer be hurt by it.

Dealing with pupil behaviour

The mistaken goals outlined above are very useful for interpreting the inappropriate behaviour of pupils, but per se do not tell you what to do. In dealing with unacceptable behaviour, I will outline 11 steps, all of which need to be taken, before applying each to a hypothetical Category D pupil called Ryan. The first seven of these can be reasonably expected from a classroom teacher. The remaining four, however, are more 'therapeutic' and may require the assistance of a qualified counsellor or psychologist.

1. Fight your first impulse (try to understand that the pupil is hurting inside).
2. Encourage the pupil at every opportunity.
3. Separate the deed from the doer. Express a liking for the pupil while still applying logical consequences.
4. Show an awareness of some 'skill' the pupil believes he or she is good at. If possible, set up a situation where you can observe the child being competent.
5. Have the child help you in a meaningful way.
6. Show some interest in something that interests the child.
7. Modify the child's curriculum and assessment (such a child will usually be a more kinaesthetic and visual learner).
8. Collect enough data to be confident of the pupil's mistaken goal.
9. Make sure the pupil is aware of his or her mistaken goals.
10. Confront the pupil with the need to choose between his or her primary goal (being liked) and the mistaken goal.
11. During class, privately inform the child of the mistaken goal as he or she misbehaves.

1. Fight your first impulse (try to understand that the pupil is hurting inside).

No matter which of the mistaken goals a pupil such as Ryan is working towards, the last thing you should do when confronted with inappropriate behaviour is to react instinctively. There are two reasons for this. First, it will only sustain Ryan's inappropriate behaviour; it will not help to stop it. More importantly, your instinctive reaction will usually further discourage what is, in essence, not a bad or naughty pupil, but a discouraged child. It will lead to further rejection of a pupil who only behaves unacceptably because he or she feels rejected.

Essentially, a teacher who reacts to an attention-seeker with irritation and annoyance, to a power-seeker with anger or exasperation, to a revenge-seeker with fear or hurt, or to a withdrawing pupil with despair or helplessness, is just giving the junkie a fix.

> Essentially, a teacher who reacts to an attention-seeker with irritation and annoyance, to a power-seeker with anger or exasperation, to a revenge-seeker with fear or hurt, or to a withdrawing pupil with despair or helplessness, is just giving the junkie a fix.

Moreover, an unthinking response may even make matters much worse by moving an attention-seeker into power-seeking, or a power-seeker into wanting revenge, and so on. At all times, the ideal response should be calm and considered. This call for us to control our natural reactions rests on the belief that such unthinking reactions feed Ryan's underlying low self-concept.

2. Encourage the pupil at every opportunity.

Since D pupils only behave inappropriately because they feel so discouraged that they think they wouldn't gain acceptance by behaving normally, it is no surprise that a major emphasis is on giving these pupils lots of encouragement. Yet, make no mistake, it is not the behaviour that should be encouraged, but the person. In giving encouragement, not only to pupils who behave unacceptably, but to all pupils, we need to let them know that they belong, and are useful and important members of the class who can contribute in socially acceptable ways.

According to Dreikurs, it is important when talking about encouragement to distinguish between recognising achievement and recognising effort. This can be illustrated by the following example. The class is working on a geography assignment. Ryan, in contrast, is clicking his pen. His teacher may respond by saying, in an irritated manner: 'Can't you sit and get on with the work without clicking that pen. Please. Stop!

It's disturbing others.' Because the teacher has focused attention on him, Ryan feels recognised by both the teacher and the class. He sits quietly for a short time before starting again. Over time, Ryan concludes that 'when I do wrong things, I get attention. If I want to be noticed all I have to do is act inappropriately.'

A teacher who is conscious of Dreikurs' framework for understanding inappropriate behaviour will feel irritated, but believe that Ryan is attention-seeking. The last thing he or she wants to do is reinforce Ryan's attention-seeking behaviour. Consequently, the teacher keeps talking, moves quietly alongside Ryan, takes the pen, and quietly places it on the desk. Ryan gets little attention, does not feel recognised, and concludes over time that 'I do not gain attention through misbehaviour'. Unfortunately, however, he will seek other ways of gaining recognition until additional strategies are implemented to address the low self-concept that drives his need for recognition.

Similarly, when addressing work attempted by pupils such as Ryan, you can respond appropriately or otherwise. If you react without enough thought you might say something like, 'You're working quite well Ryan, but you've got this bit wrong.' Over time, he may come to believe that he is not quite acceptable as he is and will only become so when he is competent. Comments like this one teach Ryan that he is no good at a given subject, for example Maths, and ultimately, therefore, no good at all.

Alternatively, Ryan may complete the assignment perfectly and then you might say, 'Well done, you've done a beautiful job.' Although this comment praises the pupil, it may also be interpreted in exactly the same way as the previous statement. Ryan may conclude that only as long as he can complete work perfectly, is he acceptable. This kind of thinking seems more prevalent among first-born children.

In contrast to making a pupil's approval conditional on satisfactory achievement of some task, as teachers so often do, it is important to accept children as they are, by separating their efforts and involvement in an activity from the quality of their performance. It would have been more helpful, that is, more encouraging, to Ryan if you said something like 'that's great, it's good to see you are enjoying Maths'. Encouragement of this sort gives pupils the courage to keep on trying and at the same time allows them to accept their current best efforts. As long as they keep trying, and gaining more maturity and experience, skills will develop.

Figure 7.1 contains a list of encouraging statements provided by a primary school I once worked with. The staff recommended these phrases as those they considered most helpful, based on their extensive experience. Dreikurs would probably be quite pleased with the results of their 'grounded' research. In practice, of course, the distinction between encouraging effort and encouraging achievement is usually blurred,

Phrases that show acceptance of the pupil:

I like the way you …

It seems that you are satisfied with …

Since you're not satisfied with …, what do you think you can do about it?

It seems that you enjoy …

How do you feel about what you've produced?

Phrases that show confidence in the child:

Knowing you, I'm sure that you will do it all right.

That's the way, you'll be able to …

I know you'll make a choice you'll be happy with.

That's hard but I'm sure you will figure it out.

Phrases that focus on contributions, assets and appreciation:

Thanks, you helped me a lot.

It was good of you to help with … Thanks, I really appreciate your help, it makes my job much easier.

I need your help to … so that … .

The way you … is really quite impressive.

Phrases that recognise efforts and achievements:

It looks as if you have worked really hard on … .

You've worked hard. It seems like you like to … .

That was difficult but I can see you figured it out.

I see that you are making progress with … you're already able to … .

Figure 7.1   Encouraging phrases

and in our society, recognition of the product is far more common than recognition of the process. Recent research, which involved observations of over 50 classrooms (Beaman, 2006), reported that a pupil is seven times more likely to be recognised for getting some schoolwork right than criticised for getting it wrong.

In contrast, when it comes to social responsibility, a pupil is six times more likely to have irresponsible behaviour criticised than to have responsible behaviour recognised. So you should not feel inadequate if you find it difficult to achieve Dreikurs' ideal. Nevertheless, encouraging achievement as well as effort, no matter how imperfect the product, is far better than no encouragement at all. Further, encouraging socially responsible behaviour more often than one criticises inappropriate behaviour is essential, even if not always practicable.

It is important to warn you about what might happen in the early stages of encouraging pupils who chronically behave inappropriately. Because their behaviour stems from low self-esteem, these pupils can find it hard to believe that they have found a teacher who genuinely likes and accepts them.

On one occasion, I had the experience of attempting to teach Matthew, a particularly difficult pupil. After concluding that his chronic behaviour was based on a need for attention, I offered him loads of encouragement, trying to convince him that he was not as unlikeable as he assumed. I found myself repeatedly saying to him: 'Matthew, I know you don't believe it, but you really are OK, in fact, you're a nice boy. It's only your behaviour that isn't acceptable.' In the early stages of this process, he found it necessary to test my words by behaving even worse, to see if he could force me to dislike him.

At the worst stage of testing me out, he reacted to the imposition of logical consequences by eventually storming out of the classroom shouting, 'You hate me! You hate me!' I responded to this outburst by later telling him privately what I thought was happening. He didn't think he was likeable, couldn't accept that I didn't dislike him (as he believed all the others teachers did), and was trying to test me. I told him that the next time he tried to test me I would respond by calmly saying: 'Testing … testing'. I had to use this strategy twice only before Matthew stopped his testing behaviour.

In summary, therefore, encouragement of acceptable behaviour is essential to making a pupil realise that he or she doesn't have to behave inappropriately to be recognised, and that recognition and belonging can be gained through normal acceptable behaviour. But it may be a long time before this process takes effect. What should a teacher do about a pupil's unacceptable behaviour in the meantime? I will deal with the answer to this in the next section.

3. Separate the deed from the doer. Express a liking for the pupil while still applying consequences for inappropriate behaviour.

Just as Category B and C pupils need to have their appropriate behaviour recognised, and inappropriate behaviour subjected to a series of increasingly severe consequences, so do Category D pupils. Not to apply consequences to the behaviour of a Category D pupil would be tantamount to giving the child the idea that we are thinking, 'Poor you, we can't expect more, so we won't.' It is important that Category D pupils realise that you do have faith in their ability to live up to reasonable expectations. Even though they may doubt their capacities, you should never let Category D pupils feel that you see them as less than capable, or victims to be pitied.

It is particularly important that when a Category D pupil's behaviour is addressed, it is done in a way that

> Not to apply consequences to the behaviour of a Category D pupil would be tantamount to giving the child the idea that we are thinking, 'Poor you, we can't expect more, so we won't.'

is least likely to make the pupil feel rejected. Subsequently, rather than simply say 'Ryan, you're talking. It's distracting the other pupils. Please be quiet!' you may preface such a statement with 'Ryan, you're a good kid, but you're talking …' If Ryan were young enough, you may even say, 'Ryan, I like you, but you're talking …' In private, you should also inform Ryan that when you need to respond negatively to his behaviour it does not mean that you dislike him. You may even tell him that you will give some non-verbal signal as you verbally address his behaviour (e.g. touch your ear lobe) so that he will know you still like him, even though you feel compelled to deal with his behaviour because it distracts the other kids. You may even need to tell him, 'There's nothing you can do that will make me dislike you.'

When choosing consequences you should understand clearly that any punishment that further undermines a D pupil's self-concept is probably going to prolong or increase the inappropriate behaviour. In contrast, any consequence that involves Ryan making use of his (usually) considerable kinaesthetic abilities to assist someone else is clearly a good idea. It is likely to increase his sense of self-worth and thereby reduce his need for the recognition that he gains through acting out. Some productive consequences may be assisting in the school's general office (photocopying, folding papers), helping the maintenance man (cleaning desks, fixing damaged equipment), the gardener, or even tutoring much younger children.

4. Show an awareness of some skill the pupil believes he or she is good at. If possible, set up a situation where you can observe the pupil being competent.

As explained above, according to Dreikurs Category D pupils have a low regard for themselves. In order to increase the likelihood that Ryan comes to believe that you value him, you should make the effort to observe him being competent. This may require watching the basketball during lunchtime, or visiting a Music, Art or Phys Ed lesson. It may even require selecting a topic or process for the normal curriculum just because it is within Ryan's sphere of competence, for example a PowerPoint presentation on karate.

5. Have the child help you in a meaningful way.

In order to convince Ryan that he is of value it is helpful to find a way that he can be of help. On one occasion, I asked a very challenging Category D pupil if he would agree to punch data from questionnaires into a Word file, for my later analysis. I agreed to pay him £2 an hour. Our relationship, and his classroom behaviour, improved greatly. My reduced stress level made it well worth the small investment.

6. Show some interest in something that interests the child.

Finding out what interests Ryan may not be easy. Nevertheless, it is of great significance because such information serves two purposes. First, it allows you to build Ryan's areas of interest into the curriculum, thereby increasing the likelihood that he will attend to the learning activities. Second, if for example you knew he was into technology, you could catch up with Ryan in the playground and show him that he is of value by saying something like, 'Ryan, I was thinking about buying a new TV and can't decide whether to get a plasma or LCD screen. They tell me you know about these things. What do you think is the best buy and why?'

One of the professional development activities I provide for teachers is to give them a minute to focus their mind on a particular D pupil they are teaching. I then ask them to raise their hand if they know what this pupil thinks he or she is really good at, or is genuinely interested in. On average only about 10 per cent of secondary teachers can do it. The percentage is higher among primary teachers. Unfortunately, many teachers are unaware of D pupils' expertise and interests, and until they become aware of them they can only be of limited help to such pupils.

7 Modify the pupil's curriculum and assessment (usually a more kinaesthetic/visual learner).

A number of years ago I was visiting a secondary school when the staff revolted. They refused to teach the most badly behaved pupils in their classes. The behaviour of these children was aggressive and intimidating. The staff wanted them removed from classes. Each pupil to be removed was identified by the four coordinators of the respective year level. I was curious about such pupils so gained permission to obtain copies of their progress reports. What I will now comment on is the perceived performance of the Year 8 'excluded' pupils in a range of subjects.

Of the 207 pupils in Year 8, 18 were removed from their classrooms. Although approximately 40 per cent of Year 8 were girls, all 18 excluded pupils were boys. This is consistent with the often reported observation that boys generally misbehave most in class. Table 7.1 below records their results. For each subject, pupils' progress was categorised as Excellent, Satisfactory, Borderline or Unsatisfactory.

Table 7.1 Progress reports for the most challenging 18 pupils in Year 8

	Excellent	Satisfactory	Borderline	Unsatisfactory
English	0	1	4	13
Science	0	2	5	11
SOSE	0	3	7	8
Maths	0	6	7	5
Tech.	0	6	7	5
Art	0	9	3	6
Phys Ed	4	7	2	5

The first observation to be made is that there were five pupils who received 'Unsatisfactory' for all the subjects. These pupils were currently unreachable and may have already 'divorced' their schools (Glasser, 1997). That is, they may have found school and teachers so unable to understand them and to respond to their needs that they chose to withdraw entirely. The interesting thing about the pattern of results for the remaining 13 pupils is that the more their performance required language skills, the less successful these pupils have been. Not surprisingly, when they were formally tested for language skills they averaged Year 3 reading level. They were not literate, so could not read the tests, let alone the resource material. Interestingly, they were able to perform creditably in Art and Phys Ed.

These children are not 'written word' people; they are not linguistic and logical learners. They are 'movement' and 'picture' people: in Gardener's words (Gardener, 1983), they are kinaesthetic and visual learners. Consequently, any attempt to integrate Category D pupils by modifying the curriculum will require an attempt to decrease reliance on linguistic skills and increase the significance of visual and performance skills. Assessment would also need to be based on visual output, role-plays, and so on.

Some schools have found it necessary to teach particular Category D pupils outside the normal programme. For example, the school providing the progress reports above made an off-site experience available for these Category D pupils, incorporating outdoor, interpersonal, and hands-on curriculum. Another recent example that crossed my desk had a group of Category D pupils spending ten weeks building motorbikes from wood, papier-mâché and cardboard. According to the teacher, the group used working arithmetic, measurement and costing for the maths element and for the English the pupils wrote reports at intervals about procedures and materials culminating in a final report wrapping up the whole project.

In addition to modifying instruction, it is also important to modify the types of assessment used to evaluate the performance of Category D pupils. It would be extremely frustrating, to say the least, if pupils were able to master the learning because of its kinaesthetic and visual nature, but not be able to communicate their mastery. So forms of assessment will need to be considered that emphasise less the read and written word. These may include assessments based on the production of diagrams, graphic organisers, maps, drawings, paintings, models, sculptures, videos, pictures, constructions, demonstrations, mimes or plays.

Having completed consideration of what may be termed 'instructional' or 'pedagogical' responses to the needs of Category D pupils, a more controversial set of recommendations will now be presented. These focus on therapeutic responses, which might arguably be the province of psychologists, not teachers. Nevertheless, in the interests of Category D pupils, these recommendations will be discussed, while acknowledging their problematic nature.

8. Help to change 'mistaken goals'.

There are two reasons why you should inform pupils of their mistaken understanding of the world. The first is that it can help confirm whether your assessment of the pupil's reason for behaving inappropriately is correct; that is, whether the pupil is attention-seeking, power-seeking, revenge-seeking or withdrawing. The second is that it enables pupils to become aware of their motivation and, ultimately, to realise that a pattern of unacceptable behaviour is not the way to gain the sort of recognition and feelings of belonging they really want.

You need to suggest to the pupil who is behaving inappropriately that you think you are aware of what is causing the behaviour. You then confront the pupil with the possible causes:

- The pupil wants special attention.
- The pupil wants to be boss.
- The pupil wants to hurt others as much as he or she feels hurt by them.
- The pupil wants to be left alone.

The purpose of this confrontation is to observe which proposition stimulates a reaction from the pupil, and might indicate that you have hit the nail on the head. These reactions, which are involuntary, include a mischievous 'I've been caught' smile, a hand covering the mouth or face, or even a twinkle in the eye.

In attempting to identify these signs successfully, it is important that you realise that there is a great risk of error. This is one reason why certain psychologists have discouraged me from discussing the following material with teachers. Just as it is argued that some children's behaviour is caused by poor self-esteem, the same could be said of some teachers' responses. Teachers' views of the world will also be influenced by factors such as their own sense of self-worth and experiences as a child. They may therefore see in a pupil's response something that is not there.

In psychological terms, this is known as *projection*, that is, you project your own feelings onto the pupil. For example, you may see a twinkle in the pupil's eye because you can remember how you behaved and thought in similar circumstances. You need to be aware of these possibilities and be on your guard.

There is another related difficulty for teachers who use Dreikurs' approach. As explained earlier, this approach argues that a teacher's reaction is his or her best guide to the possible motivation of the pupil; for example, power-seeking behaviour provokes anger. However, some teachers need to be very careful when evaluating their responses to a pupil's behaviour. Events in the teacher's life may generally influence their feelings and the way they are likely to react to their pupils. For example, if teachers are feeling pushed around by a controlling school administration they may be quick to interpret normal pupil behaviour as challenges to their power in the classroom. Consequently they may easily become angered. In summary, I wish to provide Dreikurs' ideas as food for thought but I do not recommend their use by all teachers.

9. Collect enough data to be confident of the pupil's mistaken goal.

According to Dreikurs it is vital that Category D pupils become aware of what motivates their inappropriate behaviour, and that it is a mistaken goal, be it seeking attention, power or revenge, or withdrawal. The reason is that they need to be forced to consider what is more important to them: to be liked and accepted, or to seek their mistaken goal at the expense of genuine acceptance. It is therefore important to find out how a potential Category D pupil acts in a range of situations, to determine if there is a pattern of behaviour that characterises one of the mistaken goals.

I recall a passing comment from a teacher of English who, when talking about a Category D pupil, said: 'I don't understand, he was absolutely disgusting in class, but last night he served me at McDonald's and he was excellent, efficient and courteous.' All I could think at the time was, 'Well, it's obvious, an English class demands linguistic and logical intelligence; McDonald's, in contrast, is a visual, interpersonal, rhythmic and kinaesthetic environment.' This pupil could cope well and feel competent in McDonald's. Therefore, rather than destroy the environment, he supported it.

Mistaken goals

Once you are confident about the likely mistaken goal driving a Category D pupil's behaviour, you should conduct a private discussion with the pupil aimed at making him or her aware of his or her 'mistaken' goals, and confronting the pupil with the need to choose between the primary goal (being liked) and the mistaken goal. Below is a transcript of a teacher's input into a possible conversation with a D pupil, with various important stages identified:

Gain involvement:

Chloe, I think I know why you ... [talked while I was talking/made noises in class/stole money/lied/etc.]. Do you want me to tell you what I think?

Confront motivation:

Could it be that you want special attention?

Could it be that you want to be boss and get your own way?

Could it be that you want to get even and hurt people as much as you feel they have hurt you?

Could it be you want to avoid showing others how stupid you feel you are?

Deny 'rational' excuses:

That's not it. It's not that you're bored, confused, tired. You just want to be noticed, to show people that they can't make you do stuff, to get even with everyone, to be left alone.

Defuse motivation:

You're right. If you act silly enough, people can't help noticing you.

Absolutely, no one can make you do anything.

There's no way they can stop you from hurting them.

If you want to avoid doing any work you certainly can.

Encourage:

You are a terrific kid.

I like you very much.

Confront belief about not being 'likeable':

I know you think I don't like you, but I do.

I think you feel that no one likes you, but you are wrong. I like you a lot.

I understand that you feel that no one likes you and maybe you even think you're not likeable, no matter how well you try to behave. You're wrong!

There's nothing you can do that will make me stop liking you. Give it your best shot.

Provide choice:

Do you want to be noticed or do you want to be liked (to have friends)? You can't have both.

Do you want to be boss or do you want to be liked? You can't have both.

Do you want to get even or do you want to be liked? You can't have both.

Do you want to be left alone or do you want to be liked? You can't have both.

Separate child and behaviour:

I think you want people to like you but you don't think they could. You're wrong!

If you changed the way you behaved, people would find it easier to like you.

It's hard to like someone who steals, hits, etc.

The only thing about you that is hard to like is the way you are choosing to behave.

If you choose to behave differently, the other kids would think differently about you.

Apply logical consequences:

Because you … we will now have to …

Highlight the mistaken goal during class:

The next time you … or … in class, rather than punish you, I will simply let you know that the reason for such behaviour is your need for attention (power, etc.) … so you can come to understand why you do it.

As indicated above, when you attempt to give unconditional acceptance to Category D pupils, they will often increase their misbehaviour to test you.

A recent example involved a girl in a Year 9 class. Her teacher conducted a discussion similar to that outlined above. He identified the pupil's goal as attention-seeking and suggested to her that although her 'friends' found such behaviour amusing, they also found it irritating. It was this type of behaviour that prevented them from really liking her. The teacher also said he was aware that the pupil might misunderstand when he felt compelled to react to her inappropriate behaviour, and assume that he didn't like her.

Consequently, the teacher identified a non-verbal signal he said he would use the next time the pupil displayed attention-seeking behaviour in class. Later in class when the pupil was behaving inappropriately, the teacher called her name and gave the signal. The pupil stopped the behaviour instantly, stood motionless for about 45 seconds then proceeded to wave her hands from side to side above her head and started yelling, 'I'm attention-seeking! I'm attention-seeking!'

When the teacher emailed me in desperation, I explained that his strategy was working and that he had to continue to expose the motive behind the pupil's behaviour. The relevant dialogue might go like this:

> I know why your behaviour is getting worse. Why you yelled and waved your hands about. You're saying to me – 'Like me, do you? I'll show you I'm not likeable.' It won't work. I do like you. Give it your best shot. I will deal with your behaviour because I have to protect the other kids' right to work and feel safe. But I will never dislike you. Why should I? You're a nice kid.

To complete the chapter I want to quote Ms Megan Moore, the principal of a school which deals exclusively with children whose behaviour is too extreme for them to be maintained in normal schools:

> And even the most apparently aggressive, defiant, oppositional child has a heart that's crying – crying for boundaries, crying for affirmation, crying for reassurance, crying for direction, crying for success …
>
> Building students' self-esteem is one of the overriding objectives of the program, and developing students' trust and giving them healthy doses of praise and affirmation are key aspects of the intervention. The students have to learn the parameters, they have to learn that the expectations are absolute and the consequences are non-emotive. (Moore, 2004)

Here Ms Moore speaks not as a theorist but as a very experienced practitioner. In doing so, she encapsulates beautifully the situation for Category D pupils as they have been represented in this chapter.

Before presenting a review of published and other research designed to evaluate the effectiveness of the sorts of techniques recommended in previous chapters, I want to reiterate an earlier comment related to the use of categories when considering pupils' behaviour. These categories are to be used only as a way of identifying the most appropriate management strategies for a respective pupil. This will allow teachers to efficiently assist pupils to modify their behaviour, moving from Category D to C, to B, to A.

8 | The Developmental Management Approach (DMA)

To summarise Chapters 1 to 7, without effective behaviour management a positive and productive classroom environment is impossible to achieve. As discussed in Chapter 1, identifying the most effective techniques for producing behaviour change and preventing the development of classroom discipline problems is a moderately stressful part of many teachers' professional lives (Fields, 1986; Hart et al., 1995; Johnson, Oswald and Adey, 1993; Lewis, 2001; Oswald et al., 1997). Some report it as a serious concern for teachers, administrators and the public (Hardman and Smith, 2003; Macciomei, 1999), and a major reason for job dissatisfaction (Liu and Meyer, 2005).

> Without effective behaviour management a positive and productive classroom environment is impossible to achieve.

Part of teacher concern is uncertainty about what approaches are most justifiable. The need for confidence regarding the impact of particular strategies is important to teachers. The ability to manage pupils effectively is a crucial component of teachers' sense of professional identity (McCormick and Shi, 1999), and 'disciplinarian' ranks third after 'leader' and 'knowledge dispenser' in the metaphors teachers give for their work (Goddard, 2000).

There is a range of classroom management strategies designed to meet the needs of pupils whose behaviour can be best described as belonging to one of four levels, designated in Chapter 2 as Categories A, B, C or D. These have been described in detail in Chapters 4 to 7 and include Hinting, Punishment (consequences), Recognition and Reward, and Discussion. It is only by assuming all pupils are operating at level A that a teacher can identify which pupils aren't. Those who aren't are then assumed to be at level B, until it is observed that rewards and consequences are not enough to stimulate responsible behaviour.

Once this is the case we assume the pupils are operating at level C, necessitating a number of one-on-one 'chats'. If and when there is still no improvement in the pupil's level of responsibility he or she is treated as a D-level pupil. I have called this approach the Developmental Management Approach (DMA). It may be useful here to give a brief summary of the techniques appropriate to each category of pupil behaviour in this approach.

Responding to Category A pupils: hinting

Non-verbal

1. Pausing
2. Moving closer to pupil
3. Looking at pupil
4. Checking pupil's work

Verbal

1. Describe the situation:

   There are a lot of kids making noise. I'm sure some kids can't hear properly.

   Most children are at their seats and ready to begin.

2. Give I-messages:

   When pupils push I get worried that someone may be hurt.

   I'm pleased to see that most pupils have brought their stuff.

3. Restate the expectations:

   I thought that we agreed that no one should distract others from their work.

   Didn't we say that everyone had a right to feel safe?

4. Ask questions:

   What are you doing?

   Is that fair?

Responding to Category B pupils: recognitions and consequences

Recognise responsible behaviour of individual pupils and the class as a whole

1. Provide non-verbal praise such as a smile, wink or nod or a specific signal (e.g. thumbs up).

2. Provide very specific verbal praise:

    Yu, thanks for working so hard today.

    It was good of you to help your classmate with that problem.

3. Communicate to others (note in diary, note to level coordinator, letter home, phone call to parents).
4. Provide special privileges, like choice over activities, 'free' time, access to a computer, or being a helper.
5. Provide material rewards like sweets or stationery.

Assertively apply a series of increasingly severe consequences for inappropriate behaviour

1. Explanation: Note body language; low-key if up close, assertive if across the room. Identify the pupil, describe the inappropriate behaviour, say why it is inappropriate by referring to the rights of other children in the class and demand responsible behaviour.

    Ahmud ... you're talking. It's disturbing others. They have a right to work. Please be quiet.

2. Reassert:

    I understand, but please be quiet ... Be quiet ... If you wish to discuss it, we can do that after the lesson or at lunchtime. Right now, please be quiet.

3. Offer choice and apply approximately four sequential steps, then isolate the pupil. For example, move the pupil to an isolation seat in the room and warn of the need for a talk later, then send out and now treat as a Category C pupil:

    Nathan, you have a choice. Either you stop talking or you will need to move to this seat ... I don't intend to force you but if you don't move then we will need to talk about it after class.

Responding to Category C pupils: one-on-one discussions

1. Welcome and seek help to deal with the 'problem':

    Good to see you. I need you to help me understand what happened in class.

2. State what the problem is, what effect it is having on others (including you) and how it makes you feel:

When you talk while I am talking, I worry that the other kids can't hear.

I'm concerned that you're coming late, because it distracts others.

3. Listen – and paraphrase pupils' facts and feelings. Reframe positively:

You seem to be saying that you need to talk as you are worried that …

So the reason you come late is … and it's not your fault.

4. Confront the pupil's argument. Try to show it is unreasonable:

So what you are saying is that because I didn't see Eric talking I shouldn't try to stop you preventing your friends from learning.

Because you were angry, you figure it's OK to hit Cleo and hurt her?

5. Get the pupil's agreement that there is a 'problem':

So you can see there's a problem.

6. Have the pupil provide a solution that meets both his or her, and your, needs. If necessary suggest some:

So what can you do about it?

How can you be sure that you can arrive on time?

Next time, rather than fight, what might you do instead?

7. Evaluate all the solutions and find one acceptable to both. Set a timetable to evaluate its effectiveness:

OK, then we'll try it until … and see how it goes.

If after three or four discussions there is no improvement in the level of responsible behaviour, consider the pupil as manifesting D-level behaviour.

Responding to Category D pupils: mistaken goals

There are two kinds of responses that need to be made to pupils exhibiting Category D behaviour. The first is instructional and the second therapeutic.

1. Instructional

- Fight your first impulse (try to understand that the pupil is hurting).
- Encourage the pupil at every opportunity.
- Separate the deed from the doer. Express a liking for the pupil while still applying logical consequences. Use consequences likely to rebuild self-concept.

- Show an awareness of some skill the pupil believes he or she is good at. If possible, set up a situation where you can observe the child being competent.
- Have the child help you in a meaningful way.
- Show some interest in something that interests the child.
- Modify the child's curriculum (usually D children are more kinaesthetic/visual/rhythmic learners).

2. Therapeutic

- Collect enough data to be confident of the pupil's mistaken goal.
- Make the pupil aware of his or her mistaken goal.
- Confront the pupil with the need to choose between his or her primary goal (being liked) and the mistaken goal.
- Inform the pupil (privately), during class, of the mistaken goal as he or she misbehaves.

Research support for the DMA

In general terms, there are at least three main philosophies on classroom discipline, each advocating particular techniques (Lewis, 1997a, 1997b; Wolfgang, 1995). Some educationalists argue that in order to promote responsibility in children, teachers need to develop clear expectations for pupil behaviour and then judiciously apply a range of rewards and recognitions for good behaviour and punishments for misbehaviour (Canter and Canter, 1996; Swinson and Cording, 2002; Swinson and Melling, 1995). Others argue that the aim can only be attained by less emphasis on pupil obedience and teacher coercion, and more on pupil self-regulation. The latter is facilitated by techniques such as negotiating, discussing and contracting (e.g. Freiberg, 1996; Pearl and Knight, 1998; Schneider, 1996; Vitto, 2003; Wade, 1997). The third orientation favours group participation and decision-making, whereby the group takes responsibility for ensuring the appropriateness of the behaviour of all its members (Edwards and Mullis, 2003; Glasser, 1984; Schneider, 1996).

In practice, however, most programmes addressing classroom behaviour management combine techniques from all three philosophies, with varying emphases. Even a behavioural programme such as Assertive Discipline, as it has developed in schools, has incorporated counselling techniques (Canter and Canter, 1996). Similarly, a heavily negotiation-oriented programme such as Stop, Think, Do includes the option of logical consequences (Beck and Horne, 1992).

The DMA outlined in Chapters 3 to 7 draws on a limited range of strategies. I have recently completed research which examines the impact of these strategies in classrooms. The results are reported as they apply to all pupils, whereas what is ideally required is an empirical study of their suitability to children exhibiting differing levels of inappropriate behaviour.

Nevertheless, the research is instructive in providing empirical support for the techniques that comprise Developmental Management. The research examined the impact of the teacher's disciplinary strategies on pupils' feelings towards the teacher, their belief that the teachers' disciplinary behaviour is justified, and the extent to which they feel distracted when teachers intervene (Lewis, 2006). The findings indicate that for all pupils, two of the five strategies discussed in Chapters 3 to 7 are very productive, two appear somewhat productive, and one has been characterised as counterproductive.

Recognition and Reward for responsible behaviour and Discussion and negotiation

The techniques seen by pupils as most useful for generating positive pupil reactions are the use of Recognition and Reward for responsible behaviour, and participation in Discussions with pupils where a negotiated outcome is achieved. The success of the latter technique is not surprising. Many educators and researchers write in support of the benefits of including pupils and negotiating with them. These techniques increase a pupil's sense of competency and belonging, which in turn leads to a decrease in misbehaviour (Anderman, 2002). According to Mitchell Beck and James Malley (1998), however, teacher–pupil interactions in many conventional classrooms do not make for a sense of belonging for pupils. This is most noticeably the case for pupils at risk (Beck and Malley, 1998) and the more challenging pupils, such as those displaying Category C and D behaviour (Ellis, Hart and Small-McGinley, 1998).

Many educators and researchers write in support of the benefits of including pupils and negotiating with them.

Given the extent to which Recognition and Reward relate to pupils' positive feelings towards the teacher, their belief that the teachers' disciplinary behaviour is more justified, and less perceived distraction when teachers intervene to respond to pupil misbehaviour, teachers should feel comfortable using techniques such as personal and group Recognition as part of a plan for Developmental Management. Such a recommendation is consistent with the views of a number of other researchers who promote recognition of appropriate behaviour (Buisson, Murdock, Reynolds and Cronin, 1995; Cavalier, Ferretti and Hodges, 1997; Swiezy, Matson and Box, 1992). As I have argued elsewhere (Lewis, 2006), one of the reasons why recognition of the appropriate behaviour of pupils may be productive is that it provides a way for a teacher to show pupils that he or she does not dislike them. It reinforces the fact that the teacher's emphasis is on facilitating responsible behaviour and the protection of rights.

It needs to be noted, nevertheless, that there are a number of research studies that have highlighted negative effects associated with the use of Recognition and Reward (Deci, Koestner and Ryan, 1999a, 1999b, 2001; Kohn, 1993, 1996). According to critics of the use of Recognition and Reward, if pupils were to be recognised for responsible behaviour their sense of competence and commitment could be undermined. Their desire to act responsibly would decrease once the motivators ceased. Ironically therefore, according to Alfie Kohn (1993), by recognising and rewarding responsible behaviour, teachers may make the pupils more dependent and obedient, but less responsible.

This argument clearly applies most readily to Category A pupils for whom provision of a tangible reward is deemed inappropriate. This is also why it is recommended in Chapter 5 that pupils displaying Category B behaviour should be encouraged to realise that although their responsible behaviour may be recognised, it is nonetheless obligatory for all pupils to respect the rights of others at all times. This is also why it is recommended to clarify that it is effort not behaviour that is being rewarded and why teachers should minimise the use of rewards for individual pupils in Category B as soon as practicable.

A comprehensive empirical examination of the claims for and against the use of reinforcements (Akin-Little, Eckert, Lovett and Little, 2004) supports the position taken here and in Chapter 5, and indicates that there is almost no downside to the use of extrinsic reinforcements when they are verbal and make reference to the pupils' social or academic competence.

In partial summary, it seems appropriate to argue, as has been done in Chapter 4, that teachers should provide reinforcement for responsible behaviours by pupils exhibiting Categories B, C and D behavioural patterns. In addition, as recommended in Chapter 6, with Category C pupils they should be prepared to discuss the negative impact the pupil's behaviour has on others. As a part of this process, the pupil's perspective would be explored and clarified and, if necessary, confronted. In addition, pupils should be encouraged to plan for a better future and to negotiate different ways of behaving in class.

The reason discussion is not recommended for Category A or B pupils is not that such techniques are not helpful but that they are generally inefficient. These pupils are able to distinguish between right and wrong and typically only require reminding of this fact.

Hinting

Hinting appears moderately successful because it relates to pupils' views that the teacher's disciplinary intervention is justified. However, once any relationship that Hinting shares with the other five discipline techniques investigated is removed, Hinting ceases to associate significantly with any of the pupils' attitudes. Consequently, there is no evidence for the independent influence of Hinting on the average pupil's belief that their teacher's classroom discipline procedures are justified. This limited effect of Hinting is consistent with the recommendation in Chapter 4, that Hinting is most applicable only to the most responsible pupils (those whose behaviour places them in Category A).

Punishment

Having established empirical support for the value of Hinting when dealing with Category A pupils, Recognition and Reward for B (C and D pupils), and Discussion for C pupils, it is instructive to consider the situation for Punishment. Although this technique is recommended as part of the DMA, it is reported in research to be of questionable value (Lewis, 2001, 2006). The circumstances surrounding Punishment indicate that once the relationship between the use of Punishment and the other five disciplinary techniques is removed it has very little 'unique' effect on pupils' outcomes. That is, it ceases to relate to the extent to which teachers' disciplinary interventions are seen as justified or distracting, although it does relate to having a negative attitude towards the teacher (Lewis, 2006). Consequently, the application of punishment, which increases in severity when resisted or ignored, may be of limited usefulness in promoting responsible pupil behaviour (Lewis, 2001, 2006).

> The application of punishment, which increases in severity when resisted or ignored, appears to be of limited usefulness in promoting responsible pupil behaviour.

Given the use of Punishment (in the form of consequences) within the DMA, I further interrogated data that had been analysed in my previous empirical studies. On the understanding that teachers' use of punishment coincides with their use of aggression (Lewis, 2001), and that any positive relationship between pupil responsibility and punishment may be cancelled out by the negative impact of aggression, additional analyses were carried out.

The relationship between Punishment and both Personal and Communal responsibility was examined while statistically correcting for any relationship between punishment and aggression. However, since it is likely that punishment may be having a different effect on the more and less challenging pupils, these analyses were performed separately for two groups of pupils.

The first comprised pupils who reported that they misbehaved at most only a little; the second group held those who said they misbehaved sometimes or often. In each case, the relationship was positive and statistically significant. However, the relationship between Punishment and Personal responsibility was almost twice as great for the pupils who misbehaved less. It was two and a half times as great for the relationship between Punishment and Communal responsibility.

These findings indicated the usefulness of calmly administered punishment in promoting responsibility among pupils who misbehave only occasionally. Since this is the main purpose for punishment in the DMA, the results justified its recommended use.

Teachers reflecting on DMA strategies

A second opportunity arose to determine empirically the potential of the techniques integral to the DMA. Four secondary schools had implemented the programme for approximately three years. I invited teachers at these schools to complete an evaluation survey that sought to obtain two kinds of information.

The first was an indication of whether strategies recommended within the DMA were implemented, and if so, whether they were maintained. The second part of the survey invited comments explaining why teachers did or did not implement and/or maintain the recommended strategies. Ninety-six teachers provided responses.

The survey asked the staff to respond to each strategy using the following key:

- Tried the strategy and *use it* on a regular basis
- Tried the strategy, it worked but have *stopped* using it now
- Tried strategy, it *didn't work*, have stopped using it
- *Didn't try* strategy.

What follows is a summary of their ratings (reported as percentages) and some analysis of their comments on each strategy. Other teachers may find it helpful to compare their own reactions with feedback from teachers who have some experience with the DMA.

Strategy: Letting all pupils know that classroom rules are there to protect their rights

Use It	Stopped	Didn't Work	Didn't Try
81	14	0	5

The reasons given by teachers for using this strategy range from a 'rules and control' orientation:

It's school policy.

because they respond well

to helping pupils develop an awareness of their own actions and their impact on others:

Reminding the pupil that the rules are there to serve them helps them to respect them.

Asking misbehaving pupils if they have the right to disturb their friends is very powerful.

and developing a positive educational environment:

because it is rational, reasonable, logical and fair

The main reason given by teachers who didn't use the strategy was that 'pupils already knew the information'.

Strategy: Recognising the appropriate behaviour of more challenging pupils

Use It	Stopped	Didn't Work	Didn't Try
79	14	3	4

Some teachers emphasised the benefits of this strategy to themselves:

I use it as I find it helps me to stay calm.

Staying calm is itself a strategy, with positive benefits for pupils as well as teachers. Others spoke of the effectiveness of the strategy in terms of managing classroom behaviour and encouraging effort:

Praise is the best way to get pupils to respond.

It's good to get them on side.

Encouragement is a very important tool and helps the more challenging pupils to perform better.

Although this can sometimes be difficult I try it as often as I can because it produces effort by those pupils and harmony in class.

It was also seen as useful in building rapport and mutual respect:

Lets pupils feel they are being treated respectfully and fairly.

Among the insightful responses were those that approached it in terms of building the self-esteem of the more challenging pupils:

> Helps them reflect on their goal, negative habits/self tasks. It's a start towards reprogramming negative self-talk with more positive.

Of teachers who didn't use the strategy, some said it was because it wasn't deemed necessary:

> not needed, as pupils' behaviour has been modified.

> I don't have challenging pupils.

or they simply forgot to do it. Others were more introspective, examining why they had experienced difficulty with this strategy:

> I find it difficult to alter my way of thinking and not to take a back step and react to secondary behaviours.

Strategy: Remaining calm when dealing with misbehaviour

Use It	Stopped	Didn't Work	Didn't Try
85	11	3	0

Many teachers who used this strategy emphasised maintaining rapport:

> It helps maintain your relationships with the pupil, keeps them in the adult state; you can reach them more.

or as a way to avoid escalating/exacerbating situations:

> to not amplify the situation and make it worse.

> It calms pupils down instead of firing them up.

> If I remain calm and use a caring and understanding voice this calms pupils.

It was also seen as the way to ensure a reasonable and fair outcome:

> because I am the adult and it is my responsibility to keep a cool head so that I can be fair.

> Remaining calm is really important to enable you to keep perspective and rational thought in dealing with misbehaviour.

Other comments related to this are teachers' need to feel in control of themselves, and reduce the level of stress they experience:

Pupils are able to respond appropriately to your demands and you feel in control.

I feel less stressed and in control and kids don't get satisfaction from pushing my buttons.

to keep stress levels down – I don't want to work in a negative environment.

It helps me so that I don't lose my head.

It is also seen as effective in altering behaviour:

Usually this gets better results – pupils respond in a more positive manner rather than getting aggressive.

and as an efficient strategy:

It shows that inappropriate behaviour can be eliminated without too much fuss.

The difficulty of consistently implementing this strategy is evident in the reasons given for not using it. Some teachers blamed the situation or pupils:

I can find this really difficult … especially with children being dis-respectful.

Being calm is often too difficult when you are being constantly challenged.

Others saw it as too hard to do when they were under stress themselves, for example tired or ill:

As to remembering to use the strategy – it depends on how tired or run down I'm feeling.

Sometimes when I am tired I still resort to old habits, so I have to keep trying.

The level of stress teachers experience in dealing with challenging pupils is apparent in the responses relating to controlling their own emotions:

I use it and it does work, but sometimes I get very upset and do not always remain calm.

Can't yet always stay as calm as I would like – I'm no saint and my patience is still tried occasionally.

Hard to remember to do it.

I try to do this but I still get sucked in, then I say to myself I am not going to do it that way again.

Sometimes it works.

I still do get a bit worked up sometimes but turn the anger into some kind of a joke then go back to the rules.

It's difficult to remain calm when multiple challenging pupils are present in each class.

I try to use it. It works so much better than getting angry. I do get angry sometimes though, and I can feel straight away when I have blown it.

I try hard to stay calm. Sometimes I do find it hard but I am still using the strategy as much as I can.

In contrast with this, teachers with a control orientation saw it as simply ineffective:

It will not work for some pupils who interpret this approach as a weakness or even tolerance.

Doesn't always work. Some pupils respond well, others don't pay attention.

Strategy: Being critical of misbehaviour, not the pupil

Use It	Stopped	Didn't Work	Didn't Try
93	4	0	3

A very high proportion of teachers responded positively to this strategy, emphasising the importance of distinguishing between pupils and their behaviour:

People are not the problem, their behaviour is the problem; people have the option as to how they behave.

or arguing that modelling appropriate behaviour is important:

It helps teach them about appropriate behaviour.

Pupils can see how modifying behaviour can occur, rather than personalise the issue.

Others valued the strategy in terms of maintaining their relationships with pupils:

Keeps relationships at a level where discussions can take place.

Important in maintaining pupil relationships with me.

This strategy appealed also to those teachers who stressed the importance of maintaining pupils' self-esteem:

Criticising behaviour rather than the pupils reduces the chance for lowered self-esteem in the pupils.

It's only the behaviour that is poor. I don't want the pupil to feel bad.

or thought in terms of power relationships and pupil rights:

We have no right to use sarcasm or put-downs – that's all about power playing.

This is only fair.

Others recognised its efficiency:

It's always more productive.

It seems to result in having calmer and more productive conversations with pupils.

Teachers who did not use the strategy said it was because they find it hard to separate the pupil from the behaviour, they revert to their old ways, or:

It doesn't always work as the pupil does not recognise [his or her] error.

Strategy: Using a series of increasingly severe consequences for misbehaviour

Use It	Stopped	Didn't Work	Didn't Try
80	10	1	10

Teachers use this strategy because it is perceived as 'working', that is, being effective in achieving behavioural change:

It works well and hopefully we never reach the more severe consequences.

It works – pupils respond after being moved to another seat.

It works well and pupils' behaviour improves halfway through the stages of the process.

It also demonstrates that there are consequences for inappropriate behaviour:

> It shows that, in life, inappropriate behaviours have consequences that increase in steps.

> This emphasises the inevitability of bad consequences for bad behaviour.

The strategy is also appreciated because of its consistency – pupils know (and understand) what to expect:

> The children know I will be consistent and they won't push it.

> They know what's coming and argue less.

It also speaks to pupils' expectations of fairness:

> The pupils have a strong sense of fairness and justice – they don't like you pulling consequences out of a hat.

> It provides a sense of fairness to pupils and allows pupils to have opportunity to change before facing serious consequences.

Other teachers emphasised the opportunity created by this strategy for pupil choice/input in the process and for taking responsibility for their own actions:

> Pupils know what to expect and make a choice – it becomes a choice and not a punishment.

In contrast, some teachers emphasised rules and control:

> If you back down pupils interpret this to mean they can and will get away with bad behaviour.

> I use this strategy – following the discipline policy.

> I go through the school procedure for misbehaviour.

Of teachers who did not use this strategy, some said it was because they were inconsistent in applying it:

> I give too many warnings.

> I send pupils straight to Admin.

Physical space poses a problem in some classrooms:

> I am trying to use the strategy, but it is difficult to move through the steps in very small classrooms where there is not room to move a pupil. Often the only choice is to swap one child with another one. This is very disruptive.

Others said they preferred other strategies:

> It works well for some but others want to be exited so I don't use it on those.

> I prefer to negotiate the next step rather than move to a 'severe' consequence.

Some emphasised the importance of dealing with pupils as individuals, as the consequences imposed may not have the desired effect:

> I find I need to come up with a variety of consequences – pupils are a very diverse group and not all severe consequences have the desired effect.

> Some pupils play the system, which is difficult.

Strategy: Exiting the pupils who continue to act inappropriately

Use It	Stopped	Didn't Work	Didn't Try
73	10	1	17

Some teachers use this strategy because they perceive that isolation is effective:

> Pupils don't like not getting any attention and being away from the grade.

> Exiting pupils who continue to act inappropriately gives them a jolt and gives you a breather to gather your thoughts and deal with the situation in the most appropriate way when the pupil returns.

They can also see it as allowing the pupil time to calm down and think about improving their subsequent behaviour:

> It can remove the behaviour from the room and give the pupil a chance to calm down.

> It breaks the behaviour pattern, removes the distraction for other pupils and allows time to reflect before calm discussion later.

> It seems to work with most pupils, who re-enter the class for the following lessons, showing some improvement.

> A difficult pupil often needs to be separated from the rest of the group – I find this is the most effective method in bringing a change in the pupil's behaviour.

Teachers may exit a pupil to avoid further disruption through the flow-on effect to other pupils:

> otherwise [the pupil] continues to muck up and this flows on to other pupils.

They may also want to demonstrate the consequences for continual disruption:

> to show that there are consequences for inappropriate behaviour.

> For some children, if a warning has no effect, there needs to be another consequence.

> It warns the middle-ground kids.

Supporting the rights of other pupils was frequently given as the reason for exiting a pupil:

> The other pupils are relieved when the disruptive pupil is finally exited.

> It allows others to work and have my attention.

> It gives good kids the opportunity to do good work uninterrupted.

> It enables me to work with the ones who want to work.

> Teaching and learning can go on without too much disruption.

Some saw it as a strategy for using their time efficiently:

> I have to continue with my teaching peacefully rather than wasting too much time with inappropriate behaviour.

The responses of others indicated that for them it was a matter of following school policy, which ensured consistency:

> This is school policy.

> It maintains consistency.

> It allows for consistency in the classroom management process.

There was a higher percentage of teachers who had not tried this strategy than for most of the other strategies. Some of these said it was because they had not needed to exit a pupil, or prior steps in the discipline process were effective:

> I haven't got to this point this year.

> Pupils usually respond to the other steps and this one is now not needed.

Others expressed their reluctance to use it, or their preference for an alternative:

> I feel exiting pupils makes them despise you – having a discussion on their negative behaviour is more appropriate.

> I'm trying to use this strategy but I don't like to keep on and on exiting the same pupil. If their behaviour has improved but is still disruptive I've tried to keep the pupil in. It's difficult to know what to do.

> I try to deal with each pupil on my own – when I have exited pupils it is for constant or serious misbehaviour.

> I only rarely use this strategy – it's better for pupils to see you sort issues out.

Another group did not use it because they saw it as ineffective; it did not lead to a change in pupil behaviour:

> Some pupils were never followed up and the consequences were never severe enough – it doesn't work.

> In itself, it does not have any effect on the pupil.

Strategy: Talking with pupils who are isolated, or exited from class, rather than having another staff member talk with them

Use It	Stopped	Didn't Work	Didn't Try
89	4	0	6

Maintaining or building rapport with a pupil was the key factor for many teachers who used this strategy:

> to help to build relationships with pupils – to ensure pupils understand that it is their behaviour I am punishing, not the pupil.

> By talking to pupils who are exited you are able to gain a better understanding of what is happening for the pupil.

> It is more effective if I do it; it means more to the pupil.

Responsibility was another:

> I always try to handle the problem myself.

> It is MY pupil.

> The pupils are my responsibility and I have to establish a working relationship with them.

I like to maintain control, unless the situation is very serious.

This strategy was also seen as important in reinforcing or controlling pupil behaviour:

It is important that a dialogue occurs so that next lesson there are no issues.

It is important to discuss issues with pupils personally, to maintain control of pupil management.

Again, some phrased their response in terms of school policy:

It is part of our school time-out policy.

Teachers who did not use the strategy said it was because it did not lead to change in behaviour:

I don't feel any change in result.

I found it was not effective – the pupil continued after a while.

Teachers also mentioned time constraints:

difficult to find time.

I use it when I can but don't always have the time.

or lack of confidence:

don't feel confident enough to speak to them, feel like I'll say the wrong thing and escalate the situation.

In some schools this follow-up talking with the pupil was seen as the responsibility of coordinators:

Coordinators have been doing this for me, for pupils who are exited from class. As a new teacher, it is very time-consuming. Also pupils are misbehaving in other classes so the Coordinator is mostly giving punishments.

In our sub-school the coordinators do it all and then let you know.

Strategy: Communicating to the more difficult pupils an awareness of their competencies and/or interests

Use It	Stopped	Didn't Work	Didn't Try
81	11	1	6

Building connections with the pupil was very important:

I will also talk to him about what he did on the weekend and incorporate it.

I am always trying to find out what interests them, to form some sort of bond.

I like to know who my pupils are – it gives us something to talk about in detention.

This was partly to understand the pupil, partly to demonstrate care and support:

It builds a relationship, shows you're interested and care.

Shows you respect what the child is up to – they respect you more.

Builds trust between us, and respect.

to build relationship to enhance communication.

partly a way of personalising curriculum for all kids but also to show kids that you really know them, therefore that you care.

Some teachers emphasised the need to build the pupils' self-esteem, to show them that they have strengths:

It makes them feel good and they often can't see the things that they are good at.

Looking at positives helps them to have confidence in themselves.

The behaviour is often attention-seeking, suggesting that self-esteem needs building up.

When I work in a classroom with difficult children I always do this so their relationships, self-esteem and confidence will continue to grow.

It's very important to build their self-esteem and to get them to think that there's someone who doesn't actually think 'that kid's a pain in the ass'.

This enhances the pupils' motivation and achievement:

positive reinforcement of positive actions and competencies, pupil beginning to have a sense of positive achievement

Works really well as pupils can see that they are good at things and just need to try other things.

It is also a strategy to improve behaviour:

As Coordinator I utilise this often to attempt to gain improvement in general class behaviour.

I try to get them on side so it's easier to appeal to them.

Reasons for not using this strategy are various. They include being too busy, or too slack, even though teachers regard it as an important strategy:

I haven't made a serious attempt at this – flat out dealing with the other issues.

Time is the defining factor, there is never enough.

Need to do it more.

I can often slack in this. I could do this much more often.

Others believed it did not work:

These children often just don't want to listen or will not listen.

I tried at the beginning but didn't see any point when the pupil exhibited consistently negative behaviour.

I found it was not effective: the pupil continued after a while.

This works infrequently – like the weather – although I use it.

They laugh at you. Not all their behaviour is acting out problems; to many of them this is a sport.

This works well in most cases. However, some difficult pupils will not respond positively if this sort of communication is made in front of the whole class.

I have stopped using it because discussion with some pupils would be repetitive.

Strategy: Building a quality relationship with the more difficult pupils (e.g. seeking their help)

Use It	Stopped	Didn't Work	Didn't Try
71	20	3	6

Quite a number of teachers had tried this strategy but had stopped using it, while some had not tried it. Those who were not using it said they found it challenging and it had not been successful, it was too time-consuming, or it required a consistent commitment that was difficult to maintain within the competing demands of teaching:

It is challenging. Sometimes it works, sometimes they don't want to know me.

I have done this but not 100 per cent effectively – some respond, some don't.

It has little or no effect on their attitude or performance.

Some pupils resist this and I have not been successful in achieving quality relationships with it.

I use it only occasionally. Time's a factor here.

There's a limit to how much time you can put in for someone you see a few times a week.

I have used this strategy but find it difficult to spend enough time to build relationships.

I have sometimes used it and it would be good to do more of this.

It's just dropped out of my consciousness. I'm preoccupied with the other demands of teaching in and out of class.

Those who continued to use the strategy said it gives the pupil a role and connects them:

All pupils are given jobs, so they feel important and recognised among their peers.

Keeps them busy, makes them connect with the class, shows value.

Giving them some sense of responsibility makes difficult pupils feel valued and could lead to improved behaviour.

Helps develop leadership and responsibility.

I usually enlist the help of pupils who are hard to control. They cooperate well and start seeing me as a mate.

Increasing the pupil's connectedness was seen as increasing their willingness to work:

If a child feels that you care about them, they are more willing to make an effort for you.

Sometimes the thing that forms the relationship is something you could never have thought of, for example I collect the jigsaw dinosaurs from chip packets – a difficult pupil now collects them for me and we are mates. He now completes his work.

Improving communication was another outcome mentioned:

> I find that you will gain their respect and they will communicate with you much better.

> They're more likely to listen to what you say if they trust you and think you like them.

This made them more likely to cooperate and/or resist misbehaving:

> They are more willing to cooperate and learn.

> The pupil responds in a positive and less aggressive manner.

Because pupils require support,

> very important to help build supportive strategies for the pupil

it was seen as providing positive attention and increasing self-esteem:

> It works well. They seem to get the attention they need without having to find it by acting out.

> If you find a task that a pupil is good at, it helps you develop a relationship with them and makes them feel needed or wanted.

> Positive reinforcement makes them feel good about themselves.

The teacher also benefits by understanding the pupil better:

> I listen to why they are behaving as they are, their reasons, try to make some sense of it.

> Understanding them certainly helps when I need to try to comprehend their behaviour.

> I like to get to know the whole person, not just their bad pupil persona.

Most importantly, the teachers who used it said it works, eventually:

> I always keep trying because it leaves the door open and in years to come pupils remember. They ease back and tell you they appreciated it even if they didn't show it at the time.

Strategy: Trying to engage the more difficult pupils by adjusting curriculum delivery (e.g. including greater pupil interaction, movement, visuals)

Use It	Stopped	Didn't Work	Didn't Try
79	12	4	4

Teachers who found that this strategy worked for them said it gives the pupil an experience of success and increases motivation:

> Success for pupils with difficulties is very important as it enhances self-esteem.

> where possible, modifying expectations, tasks, helping with organisation and management

> Finding areas where difficult pupils feel they can achieve positive results will make them feel better about their learning.

> It's common sense – try to get them on track and some early success to build on so that the situation is not complicated by their avoidance of failure behaviour.

Furthermore, some teachers said pupils were also less likely to be difficult if they are engaged in the learning experience:

> If I make the curriculum exciting the difficult pupils are not so difficult.

> I do use this strategy without singling them out. I achieve this by incorporating visuals, movement etc. as a whole class focus. I just find that it really works well for those pupils who need that kind of stimulus or are more challenging.

> If they are all engaged it makes life easier for everyone in the classroom.

Meeting individual learning needs of pupils was part of this:

> Different courses for different horses. I use lots of visual prompts, MI stuff, auditory, music, tactile/kinaesthetic.

> I plan lessons to appeal to all levels.

> It works – everyone learns differently.

Those teachers who did not use the strategy said that it doesn't work:

> Some pupils just don't want to be engaged no matter how much time and effort goes into what you set up.

> It hardly makes any difference – they don't want to work, so no matter what, they don't respond.

> I modified the work but the pupils still refused to cooperate.

Class sizes were seen as an issue in relation to this strategy:

> It can be difficult in a larger class, always try to differentiate curriculum.

as was the need for greater organisation, time, resources:

> Still try to use it at times but it is often hard to find the opportunity.

> It is too hard to run pracs with no cash-ola.

> I don't have a choice of resources.

> I find it very difficult to plan for the needs of all the pupils. Time is a big deterrent to this.

> It's not always easy to adjust curriculum because of photocopying expenses and lack of time.

Diversity in the classroom was seen as a complicating factor:

> It's too much to adjust for learning styles as well as difficult pupils.

> I try and use it but it's not always possible due to the mixture of pupils in classes.

> Regularly used for most of the class but this dumbs it down for the one-third of academic pupils as it is too slow for them.

Teachers also spoke of the need to develop the skills for this approach:

> I need to be more flexible and work outside my comfort zone.

> I'm not as flexible in this area – I feel very passionate about my subject. If they don't engage I'm disappointed but if most are with me I tend to let the few who aren't slip through the net.

> trying to do this – need more expertise in this

The simplest responses were:

> I don't want to.

> I've found personal connection outweighs mode of delivery of work.

Strategy: Providing opportunities for difficult pupils to achieve success by altering the types of assessment

Use It	Stopped	Didn't Work	Didn't Try
63	10	3	22

This strategy was the least used and the least tried. As would be expected, many of the responses were expressed in terms of the requirements of the school, curriculum, or some other form of constraint. Some teachers said they had never needed to try this strategy. Others gave more personal responses:

> I did not try this because it affects the relationship between the teacher and other pupils in the class. Modified tasks are offered only to pupils who have difficulty, not to those who are difficult.

> I'm still trying. This is a challenging one and I am trying to improve my knowledge and understanding of a broad range of assessments.

> I would like to have time to explore this option.

> I would still do this occasionally, but not often enough – lack of time.

> I have used this but find it difficult to cater for all abilities.

Some teachers said it doesn't work:

> Difficult pupils do not want to follow instructions no matter what.

> Even given different options, [difficult pupils] don't care and persist in being difficult.

Others had experienced difficulty in implementing it:

> Difficult pupils appreciate this but others want similar work and then debate starts.

Teachers who did regularly use this strategy saw it as part of catering for individual needs:

> I have to cater for what they can achieve.

> I build into my teaching a range of assessment tasks to service all pupils in the class.

> I use this because individuals learn differently, so I try and assess them on how they learn best.

or a way of building confidence/self-esteem/a sense of achievement:

> I modify work so difficult pupils can [have] some sense of achievement.

> This empowers pupils to learn and achieve success.

> Pupils need initial success to build on further success.

> Difficult pupils usually have poor literacy skills, struggle to complete tasks, so altering types of assessment helps them to stay focused.

One teacher said effort requires recognition:

> If they try and persist they deserve rewards. What did Einstein say? 'Pass them all, life will find them out!'

Comments

Overall, the data indicates that in practice, the strategies recommended within the DMA are seen by those using them as very helpful. The proportion of staff finding a given strategy useful ranges from 73 to 97 per cent, although in most cases between 5 and 20 per cent of teachers tried the strategy and found it worked but have stopped using it. This tendency for some staff to return to old and less productive habits is a cause for concern and will be addressed in the next chapter. The most challenging strategies relate to noticing when challenging pupils are behaving well and giving recognition for this, and to building quality relationships with these challenging pupils.

Many staff appeared to find it difficult to express their reasons for adopting (or not adopting, or not maintaining) approaches to classroom management. A number of respondents simply described what they did without giving a reason.

Inspection of the reasons why teachers chose to adopt strategies advocated by the DMA reveals that they found the strategies of value because they:

- provide clear, consistent and logical expectations
- empower pupils
- minimise future misbehaviour, enhance pupil self-esteem and the quality of teacher–pupil relationships
- build rapport between teacher and pupils
- aid pupil achievement and feelings of success
- meet individual learning needs.

The reasons teachers gave for choosing not to adopt strategies advocated by DMA included:

- They forget them in the hustle and bustle of the classroom.
- They find it too challenging.
- They lack time and other resources.
- Tiredness or illness make it difficult.
- They need to develop specialised knowledge or skill (particularly in relation to strategies involving curriculum design and individualised assessment).

A number of respondents suggested that they didn't use some of the strategies because they 'didn't need to'. Others indicated that they did not adopt strategies because they 'didn't work'.

Having identified how aggressive disciplinary strategies such as yelling in anger, group punishment and sarcasm may be avoided by using techniques related to the needs of pupils, one might assume it's a simple thing for all teacher aggression towards pupils to be removed from a school. Unfortunately, it's not that easy. The final chapter will consider the process of support for teachers trying to increase their use of more productive classroom management techniques.

9 | Teacher support

Development of responsible behaviour

As explained in Chapter 1, since the 1980s there has been great interest in how schools can facilitate the development of responsible behaviour in pupils, and of all the school-related factors influencing pupil responsibility, classroom management is among the most potent (Ingersoll, 1996; Lewis, 1997b, 2001). Observational studies of classrooms (e.g. Gottfredson *et al.*, 1989; Kounin, 1970) and surveys of teachers, pupils and parents (e.g. Hyman and Snook, 2000; Lewis, 2001, 2006; Lewis *et al.*, 2005, 2007) have been used to identify the most effective strategies for teachers in achieving responsible pupil behaviour.

As was also discussed in the same chapter, when teachers verbally abuse children, humiliate them by the use of sarcasm, frequently and repeatedly send them out of class, or impose arbitrary and harsh punishments, their pupils are more likely to be absent from school. They are also more likely to be disengaged from schooling, lacking in interest or motivation, and experiencing a range of feelings such as guilt, resentment or rebelliousness (Hyman and Snook, 2000; Lewis, 2001, 2006; Lewis *et al.*, 2007).

In contrast, pupils who are more responsible have a teacher who is more likely to discuss misbehaviour with them, involve them in decision-making, hint when they misbehave, and recognise their appropriate behaviour. The results are consistent across all levels of schooling (Lewis, 2001) and across three national settings (Lewis *et al.*, 2005, 2007). Other studies have shown that pupils who describe their teachers as displaying anger, and using various forms of aggressive behaviour, become less interested in the subjects being taught (Henderson, Fisher and Fraser, 2000; Lewis and Lovegrove, 1988).

However, as indicated in the last chapter, knowing about a technical classroom management repertoire, like that outlined in Chapters 4 to 7, is not sufficient. Teachers may wish to use educationally justifiable models of management, in which they act as role models for responsible behaviour (Fenstermacher, 2001). But they also want to quickly gain the amount of order that is essential if classroom learning is to take place (Barton, Coley and Wenglinsky, 1998). What the teacher sees as best practice may also be at odds with the way he or she was treated in childhood.

As highlighted in Chapter 1, classroom discipline is a well-documented source of teacher stress (e.g. Borg, Riding and Falzon, 1991; Friedman, 1995, 2006; Lewis, 1999b). Significantly, the teachers most likely to be using counter-productive discipline techniques are those less likely to ask for help (Lewis, 1999b). They often feel unsupported by their colleagues, and the issue is seen as threatening to their status and career. Bill Rogers' research (2002) shows that even when other teachers want to assist there remains a perceived risk in asking for or giving support.

It has been shown that improvements in classroom management can be stimulated by the provision of focused, short-term teacher training. However, while behavioural change lasting for a few weeks or months is possible to achieve, relatively few individuals maintain a more lasting behaviour change (Emmer and Aussiker, 1990; Hart *et al.*, 1995), particularly when it comes to dealing with the more challenging pupils. Currently therefore, a central research question is how to produce *sustainable* improvement in teachers' classroom management behaviour.

What will be outlined in this chapter is a whole-school approach to supporting teachers attempting change in classroom management behaviour. It is premised on the assumption that 'creating professional work environments where teachers feel supported by other professionals and school leaders in relation to their own needs for competence, autonomy, and quality relationships, is essential to their decision to create these conditions for students' (Roeser, Eccles and Sameroff, 2000, p. 466).

> 'Creating professional work environments where teachers feel supported by other professionals and school leaders ... is essential to their decision to create these conditions for pupils.'

The need for teacher support

Recent research on professional development (PD) is critical of most PD programmes. The criticism relates to the short-term nature of the PD, which is generally found to be ineffective. The report states that 'ensuring opportunities for every teacher to receive "at the elbow" support and coaching during the difficult phase of implementing significant change in the classroom is a feature of effective programs' (Ingvarson, 2005).

Having identified a range of classroom management strategies in Chapters 4 to 7 and established their usefulness in Chapter 8, in the

Strategies of Developmental Classroom Management

Below are 14 suggestions for teachers to consider when working with children's challenging behaviour. The aim is to avoid the use of (need for) aggressive disciplinary techniques like yelling in anger, attacking sarcasm, group punishment etc.

1. Letting all pupils know that expectations for appropriate classroom behaviour are based on the rights of other pupils to work and to feel safe.

2. Noticing when the more challenging pupils respect other pupils' rights and saying something nice or providing some other kind of recognition. Recognising the effort required to act responsibly, rather than the behaviour itself.

3. Minimising the use of rewards for effort by talking to pupils about the need for rights and responsibilities so that the effort they require to act responsibly is reduced. Nevertheless, trying to balance reward and punishment for all pupils.

4. Remaining calm when dealing with misbehaviour.

5. Hinting when pupils aren't acting responsibly. Moving from less interventional techniques (pausing, moving closer, checking work) to verbal hints aimed at pupil responsibility).

6. Explaining why misbehaviour is unfair to other pupils before telling pupils how to behave properly or giving them consequences.

7. Using a series of increasingly severe consequences for misbehaviour when pupils argue or repeat the misbehaviour.

8. Exiting pupils who continue to act inappropriately

9. Talking with pupils who are isolated, or exited from class, rather than having another staff member talk with them.

10. Emphasising that pupils not only need to act appropriately (Personal responsibility), but also need to encourage their classmates to act appropriately (Communal responsibility). For example, rewarding and punishing Communal responsibility more heavily than Personal, discussing Communal responsibility when setting up expectations for appropriate behaviour, and when Hinting.

11. Communicating to the more difficult pupils an awareness of their competencies and/or interests.

12. Building a quality relationship with the more difficult pupils (e.g. seeking their help, watching them be competent at lunchtime).

13. Trying to engage the more difficult pupils by adjusting curriculum delivery (e.g. including greater pupil interaction, movement, visuals).

14. Trying to give the more difficult pupils a greater chance to do well on assessments by including more visual and kinaesthetic tests like drawing posters, making models and drama).

OTHER [Please specify.]

Understanding Pupil Behaviour Copyright © Lewis 2009

Figure 9.1   Strategies of developmental classroom management

remainder of this chapter I will outline and justify the support component of the DMA. I will also report some more data from the 96 teachers who have been involved in this school-based approach.

The support aspect of the DMA combines three key elements:

1. Identifying a range of helpful classroom management strategies.
2. Identifying a clear set of behaviours to indicate teachers in need of support.
3. Establishing and maintaining a clear, functional support structure for teachers, not dependent on administrative staff. This may include collegial teams or a 'buddy'.

Teachers within a number of schools have worked collaboratively with the author for up to nine years to implement and maintain a school-wide system of support for colleagues attempting to improve the effectiveness of their classroom management. In general the kind of management strategies they are trying to avoid include a raised angry voice, the use of sarcasm, name-calling, arbitrary and excessive punishment, group punishments, sending pupils out without intermediate steps, or sending challenging pupils to other teachers to be fixed.

Identifying teachers who may need support could be deemed unethical unless they can be offered effective assistance to enable them to improve. To highlight some classroom management techniques that may be of assistance to teachers within a particular school, strategies extracted from the DMA are offered to staff for comment. Figure 9.1 (page 140) outlines the form of evaluation undertaken by staff. In general, out of the many occasions this has been done, teachers supported all but one or two of the strategies.

Once a teacher in need of support is identified, discussions between the teacher seeking support and supportive colleagues focus on which of the 14 strategies might be of assistance. They then work out ways of having the teacher systematically implement the strategies identified. They also decide how to give feedback to the teacher on how well they have been implemented and their impact on pupils.

Setting up a support system

Some schools implementing the DMA have chosen to set up support systems for staff by focusing on a particularly challenging class. Then, all teachers of that class meet to discuss the strategies of management recommended as part of the DMA. Once some are identified as potentially useful, staff working with the challenging class meet regularly to report on their implementation and success. With agreement, they can observe each other employing the techniques and offer co-collegial coaching.

An alternative approach, adopted by other schools, has required each staff member in a school to identify a 'buddy'. Buddies are colleagues

Please indicate below who you would prefer to speak with you if it is thought that you might need some sort of support. Your colleagues would then be expected to pass any concern on to this 'contact' person.

If there were a need I would wish _____ to contact me.

The sort of support that could be useful would be:
(Please tick one or more, and, if possible, write in the name of the person you wish to provide the support.)

1. Having a place to put a difficult pupil until I can talk to him or her.
   [Person to provide support:_____].
2. Having someone I can trust to listen to me talk about how I am feeling.
   [Person to provide support:_____].
3. Have more time so I am able to talk through the issue with a pupil.
   [Person to provide support:_____].
4. Have someone I trust listen to me talk about the techniques I am using with the pupil. [Person to provide support:_____].
5. Get someone to 'model' techniques that might work with this pupil.
   [Person to provide support:_____].
6. Get advice on who the pupil can be referred to.
   [Person to provide support:_____].
7. Have someone watch me working with the pupil and offer advice on what else to do. [Person to provide support:_____].
8. Get more information about classroom management techniques.
   [Person to provide support:_____].
9. Get information on the pupil's behaviour in other settings.
   [Person to provide support:_____].
10. Have someone mediate between me and the pupil.
   [Person to provide support:_____].
11. Get more information on what works and doesn't work in other classes with this pupil. [Person to provide support:_____].

OTHER [Please specify.]

What sort of support would you be willing to offer your colleagues?

Please write your name clearly: _____

Understanding Pupils Behaviour Copyright © Lewis 2009

Figure 9.2   Request for staff to nominate 'buddies'

named by each staff member who are expected to approach that staff member exhibiting trigger behaviour and who therefore may be in need of support. To identify a staff member who could act as a buddy, all staff are asked to complete a form like that shown in Figure 9.2 (page 142).

Despite concerns from some teachers in the schools using the DMA that only a few teachers would be chosen as buddies, there have only been a few occasions where a potential buddy was forced to decline a nomination because of multiple nominations. Obviously not all staff need a buddy, but to avoid the possibility of having teachers feel singled out if they were to participate in the buddy process, all staff are invited to take part.

Once each teacher's buddy is identified and recorded, the next stage of the process, identification of triggers for support, is undertaken.

There are two kinds of triggers that activate support for teachers. The first take the form of aggressive classroom management techniques such as:

- aggressive disciplinary behaviour
- yelling in anger at misbehaving pupils
- using sarcasm to control misbehaviour
- calling misbehaving pupils names (like 'idiot')
- punishing pupils without giving a warning
- not recognising the good behaviour of 'difficult' pupils
- sending pupils out of class without intervening 'steps'
- regularly sending more than two pupils out of class
- keeping the class in when only some kids misbehaved.

Techniques such as these are discussed by school staff, and those agreed upon by at least 80 per cent become formal triggers.

The second set of indicators focuses on what teachers might *not* be doing rather than what they *are* doing. Some staff can avoid manifesting aggressive disciplinary techniques by 'copping out' of their classroom management responsibilities. These responsibilities relate to pursuing minimal expectations for pupil classroom behaviour that staff agree are crucial to the culture of their school and that all staff in the school are expected to police.

How teachers ensure that pupils live up to these expectations is a personal decision. It might take the form of personal intervention or just informing an appropriate staff member. However, failure to respond in any form when pupils ignore these expectations is taken by colleagues as a sign that the teacher may require support. This is only when at least 80 per cent of staff agree that such expectations are essential for pupils. The assumption is made that the teacher wanted to act responsibly and had the knowledge and skills necessary to ensure that pupils lived up to minimal expectations. In general, the sorts of expectations for pupils that teachers have highlighted relate to respectful communication, respect for property and no intentional disruption of learning.

Using these two sets of triggers for support is an essential aspect of the DMA. Clearly there is a difference between support and accountability. It is necessary for staff to agree that the triggers are triggers for concern about the welfare of a colleague, not triggers for a performance review or evaluation. This is easy to say, but it takes a long time to permeate some school cultures.

As discussed in Chapter 1, there are elements of risk in offering teachers professional development programmes. Teachers most challenged by classroom management (as many as 30%) may actually be damaged by the process of attempting change. Expectations are raised by the skills development programme and initial success, but when they find they cannot maintain the behavioural change, they may become self-critical, depressed, or resort to denial of the problem, making later efforts to change more difficult (Lewis, 1999b).

It has already been noted that teachers who are more concerned about their inability to discipline pupils in the way they would prefer are less likely to share their concerns. They are also more likely to worry and to blame themselves for getting it wrong.

Recent research (Lewis, 2008) indicates that coping strategies such as these bring about the likelihood of more teacher aggression in the classroom. Consequently, it is vital that selected buddies approach their friend when triggers are activated, rather than expect stressed staff to seek help. It may be the only way to break the cycle of more stress – more non-productive coping – more teacher aggression – more pupil mis-behaviour – more teacher stress. The question now is, what does support look like?

Characteristics of support

The first characteristic is that whatever support is, it's between the staff member and the support team or buddy and involves no one else unless the stressed teacher requests additional help. Consequently, even when a staff member is approached by a level coordinator regarding a stressed buddy, he or she is not permitted to say who suggested the possible need for support.

If the potentially stressed staff member requests it, the buddy can report in confidence that there is some sort of misunderstanding and all is well, but cannot disclose the name of the staff member concerned. The usual approach by a buddy takes an open form, for example 'How is it going in Year 9?' Teachers need to be aware that many of the things they may feel inclined to say in support of a buddy may not necessarily be perceived by the buddy as helpful.

Statements identified by staff in over 20 schools as not very helpful include the following:

It's OK, there's no reason to be upset.

I'm surprised, because he's never like that for me.

Don't worry too much, life's like that.

You know what you should do.

But I can see how he could react that way because …

Oh, you poor thing.

Remember, you've only got five years to go to retirement.

Maybe you're really upset because as a child you …

Don't worry about that kid, he's just a moron.

You've got to show these kids who's boss.

Supportive statements identified by staff as more helpful include:

Just let it all out. Say exactly what happened.

So if I hear you correctly the problem seems to be … How about a beer or a cup of coffee?

Do you want to talk to someone else about it?

Is there anything I can do to help?

In addition to verbal support, teachers in schools which introduced the DMA identified a number of other useful elements of support, which were then rated using a 4-point scale; Definitely helpful, Probably helpful, Not sure and Not helpful. Table 9.1 (page 146) indicates how helpful 507 teachers in 23 schools rated these elements.

Inspection of these responses indicates the teachers believe that time to talk one on one with pupils exhibiting Category C behaviour would be very useful. It is relevant to repeat that in some of the schools using the DMA, rather than sending pupils to senior teachers, the senior teachers are called to come and hold the class while the teacher takes the Category C pupil aside for a chat.

In addition to time, teachers clearly see the advantage in having a place to put a Category C pupil until the talk can take place. Consequently, as explained earlier, in a number of schools implementing the DMA, exited Category C pupils are sent to the school's main reception area where office staff redirect them to the back of a class that differs by two year levels from their own.

Table 9.1 The usefulness of various forms of support

Elements of Support	Definitely Helpful	Probably Helpful	Not Sure	Not Helpful
Have more time so I am able to talk through the issue with a pupil.	72	23	4	2
Get information on the pupil's behaviour in other settings.	54	37	4	2
Have a place to put a difficult pupil until I can talk to him or her.	57	32	7	5
Get more information on what works and doesn't work in other classes with this pupil.	56	37	5	2
Have someone I trust listen to me talk about how I am feeling.	50	33	11	7
Get advice on who the pupil can be referred to.	49	39	8	4
Have someone I trust listen to me talk about the techniques I am using with the pupil.	48	39	10	3
Get someone to model techniques that might work with this pupil.	45	37	11	3
Get more information about classroom management techniques.	36	48	10	6
Have someone watch me working with the pupil and offer advice on what else to do.	25	39	23	12
Have someone mediate between me and the pupil.	18	35	27	19

Interestingly, these schools prefer the use of administrative staff because they have found Category C pupils more likely to cooperate with the office staff than with teachers – less legitimate power, I suspect. Other supports identified by a majority of staff as definitely helpful include a buddy to talk with, more information about the pupil's behaviour in other settings, particularly information about what management techniques work with these pupils. Very questionable supports include mediation and coaching, which no more than a quarter of teachers see as definitely helpful.

When pupils are exited, they are given a questionnaire to be completed while they are in the back of the 'sitter' class. Figure 9.3 reproduces this

You were asked to leave the classroom.

Please write the date and your year level. Circle whether you are male or female:

Date: _____   Year Level: _____   Sex: Male   Female

We would appreciate it if you could give us some idea why this has happened.

Circle letters to show why you think you are here. Be as honest as you can.

SA = strongly agree A = agree D = disagree SD = strongly disagree

1. The teacher hates me:	SA	A	D	SD
2. I distracted others from their work:	SA	A	D	SD
3. I made other people feel unsafe:	SA	A	D	SD
4. I made the teacher angry:	SA	A	D	SD
5. I argued with the teacher:	SA	A	D	SD
6. I hurt the feelings of other pupils:	SA	A	D	SD
7. I ignored the teacher's instructions:	SA	A	D	SD
8. The teacher just picks on me:	SA	A	D	SD
9. I made too much noise:	SA	A	D	SD
10. I arrived late to class:	SA	A	D	SD
11. I did not have equipment for class:	SA	A	D	SD

Think carefully about this teacher and this subject. Would you say:

1. The teacher likes me:	SA	A	D	SD
2. I like the teacher:	SA	A	D	SD
3. I like the subject:	SA	A	D	SD
4. I am angry about being sent out:	SA	A	D	SD
5. The teacher acts unfairly:	SA	A	D	SD

Please answer the questions on the other side of this sheet.

Figure 9.3   Exit questionnaire

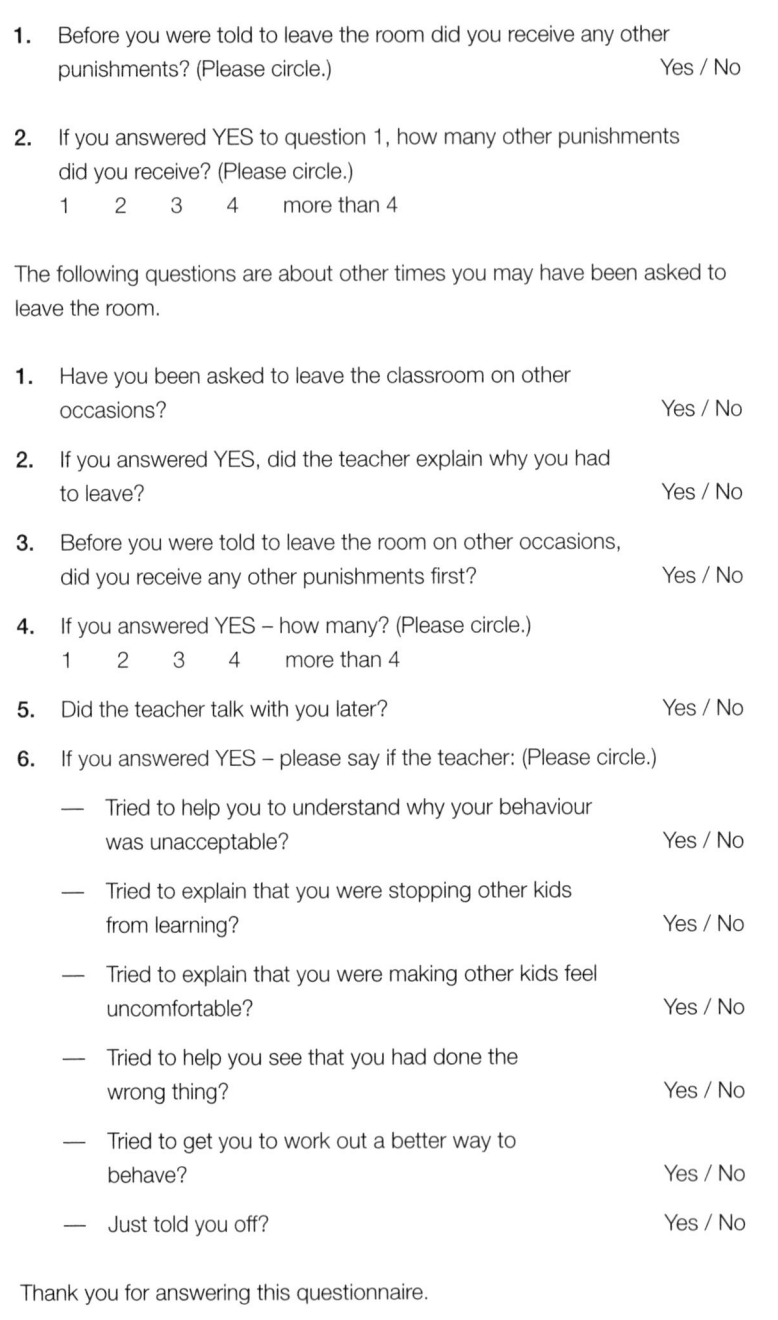

1.   Before you were told to leave the room did you receive any other
     punishments? (Please circle.)   Yes / No

2.   If you answered YES to question 1, how many other punishments
     did you receive? (Please circle.)
     1   2   3   4   more than 4

The following questions are about other times you may have been asked to
leave the room.

1.   Have you been asked to leave the classroom on other
     occasions?   Yes / No

2.   If you answered YES, did the teacher explain why you had
     to leave?   Yes / No

3.   Before you were told to leave the room on other occasions,
     did you receive any other punishments first?   Yes / No

4.   If you answered YES – how many? (Please circle.)
     1   2   3   4   more than 4

5.   Did the teacher talk with you later?   Yes / No

6.   If you answered YES – please say if the teacher: (Please circle.)

     —   Tried to help you to understand why your behaviour
         was unacceptable?   Yes / No

     —   Tried to explain that you were stopping other kids
         from learning?   Yes / No

     —   Tried to explain that you were making other kids feel
         uncomfortable?   Yes / No

     —   Tried to help you see that you had done the
         wrong thing?   Yes / No

     —   Tried to get you to work out a better way to
         behave?   Yes / No

     —   Just told you off?   Yes / No

Thank you for answering this questionnaire.

Figure 9.3   Exit questionnaire (continued)

questionnaire, which provides school-wide feedback on pupils' views of why they have been exited. As a teacher more skilfully implements the DMA, it is assumed exited pupils should be able to see that the reason the teacher asked them to leave was because their behaviour interfered with the learning of other pupils or their right to feel safe. It was not because the teacher did not like them.

The questionnaire also provides feedback on whether the teacher who exited the pupil conducted a follow-up adult-to-adult discussion. This provides more data for the school. In theory, the more teachers have discussions with pupils, the clearer it becomes that the teacher's sole motive for exiting a pupil is his or her obligation to protect the learning and safety rights of other pupils.

In order to examine the experience of staff in four secondary schools which had been, in theory, implementing the support component of the DMA for at least two years, a survey of staff was carried out. The teachers in these schools were asked what sort of support (from colleagues and from the school [structures and management]) is necessary for teachers to implement the classroom management strategies of the DMA.

Necessary supports

The type of support teachers said was necessary was extracted from their written comments. Each theme is exemplified by written comments and includes the following:

1 Buddy – someone to send the pupil to

a colleague to accept the pupil when they are exited

having somewhere to send the pupils

continual placing [of] difficult pupils into other classes

Buddy – etc. Another teacher to place kids with for short times

2 School-wide consistency and commitment

School and teachers need to be all in agreement.

Common language goals and approach empowers staff as a whole – increases success.

consistent approach across all coordinators

working all together as united and same front

Often get comment of 'but in Mrs … class we can'

having a shared/agreed approach with specific difficult pupils

3 Ongoing PD

practice to get up routine or language

ongoing PD

consistent refreshers, more role plays

needs to be revisited and invigorated periodically

4 Access to information via professional learning teams/ structured professional discussion

talking about strategies, sharing ideas about strategies/techniques

need to discuss progress with others who encounter the same pupils

discussion of strategies

discussion of ideas

discussing/sharing ideas for rewards and creative consequences

sharing of ideas/plans/strategies that did/don't work

more sharing of ideas for difficult pupils

5 Communication

follow-up on incidents, letting me know if someone in my grade is involved in an incident

background info on pupils

maintaining profile of this style of approach

follow-up, communication about pupils' issues

6 Collegial support

confidential sounding boards

a listening ear

7 Mentoring/modelling

mentoring

modelling

8 Observation/feedback

observation

positive feedback

Some teachers require another individual in class to observe, provide feedback and offer suggestions on alternative strategies.

Observation frequent. Non-judgmental. Collaboratively critical.

9 Structures/transparent processes and rules

policies, procedures

people to coordinate

more time needs to be spent on simplifying processes in schools to allow for these changes to be made

a structured process, a consistent flow of procedures

10 Resources/time

time-out area

more time, less pupils

time and space to conduct conversations

coordinators and Welfare staff with sufficient time to handle referrals; sufficient space in the week to be able to modify assessment tasks

more resources

11 Induction

revisit strategies to inform new staff members

12 Opportunities for relationship-building

opportunities to get to know pupils (and form relationships) outside their classroom

time allowances for relationship-building – whole-school events to provide stimulus

13 Curriculum support

differentiated curriculum, curriculum committee to approve

14 Parental support

support from coordinators/parents

whole-school community support

full support [from] parents

15 Leadership/management back-up

support from admin and level coordinators

whole-school community support

full support [from] colleagues, principal

Welfare Coordinator and outside agencies and admin support also work-ing as consistent group bringing into line those that aren't consistent

coherent and strong support at Coordinator and Welfare level

more belief in what the teacher says as opposed to the pupil's point of view

support from the management/principal team, coordinators and leader-ship teams in terms of ideas, enforcement, contacting parents, etc.

16 Building social connections

Friday night drinks and talk

Received support

Having established what was perceived as necessary, teachers rated the level of support received. To indicate the extent to support, teachers were given four alternatives and asked to choose one. The alternatives were No Support, Little, Some, and Full Support. Once they had responded, teachers were asked to explain their selection.

Level of collegial support received

No Support	Little Support	Some Support	Full Support
2%	8%	59%	30%

The range of justifications for selecting full support included receiving 'Advice from colleagues' and participating in 'Staff discussions':

I always get support from the school and the teachers. They always make themselves available if I need advice.

A number of colleagues gave me a variety of strategies to use with tougher pupils.

Peer support person offered assistance with ideas and feedback. Support from team members through discussion and ideas and feedback.

Usually when I am worried about something happening in my class I talk about it with my colleagues … and ask what I should do or just debrief. This usually helps.

great support with staff helping each other, being there for each other

discuss problematic situations and exchange ideas to cope with them

The use of a 'Buddy system' was also considered, as was 'Consistency' and 'Role modelling':

full support from my buddy

I put pupils in other staff members' classes and vice versa but this could be more frequent and accessible, especially for team teaching.

Colleagues are supportive by accepting exited pupils in their classrooms. They share materials but need to find a way to make this sharing more efficient.

all using same language and formed a united group

classroom management plans, however very diverse among colleagues

consistent role modelling from others

Others suggested that 'Back-up' and 'Discussion/Meetings' were crucial:

I am always backed up by the teachers.

We discussed how we were implementing the strategies at a whole-school meeting.

good support from talking and discussing strategies, but could be better

verbal discussion and comment that made me feel justified and that it was quite OK.

As was 'Transparency' in structures/processes, as well as 'Ongoing PD':

PD flowchart

We are aware of the people to go to for specific things – it is a transparent chain.

opportunity to attend whole-school PD and follow-up

The unsupported

Staff who indicated that they did not feel that support was provided suggested that:

> We have had opportunities for sharing but we are still not open enough as a whole staff because we have sceptics or non-participants who pretend to be practising positive relationships but actually are not.

> not always feasible to have a buddy given classroom and timetable arrangements

Level of administrative support received

No Support	Little Support	Some Support	Full Support
1%	8%	51%	40%

The main justifications for selecting some or full support included the 'Removal' of pupils, 'Availability', and 'Follow-up PD':

> difficult pupil removed from class for a few lessons

> depending on availability and whether they were in the school at the time

> difficult when hierarchy left the school for meetings

> Administration can be busy when you need them, but they are there when they can be.

> follow-up PD on how we are using strategies

> just discussed at a whole-school meeting

> in house PD re: Role playing conversations

Other staff discussed factors such as 'Management – advice/support', 'Structures', 'Consultation', and the delivery of 'Feedback':

> Management team are always willing to offer support.

> I feel that the school is supportive of helping me in any difficult situations. I don't feel that I have to tackle it on my own.

> leadership/management help from coordinators if needed

> especially KLA and Year Level teachers' willingness to help me to identify the problems, suggested strategies and tasks that would be achievable. Follow-up on incidents where required.

Full support has come for me a number of times when I have encountered troubles with difficult pupils and coordinators have backed me up 100 per cent.

Coordinator system/intention is excellent. Exiting procedure works smoothly most of the time. The administration is constantly trying to find systems of handling pupils who are difficult. They give these pupils tremendous support. We are still trying to get things right.

flow chart in place for consequences

PD flowchart

formal structures for negotiating classroom rights and responsibilities, time-out procedures and follow-up

a clear structure/set-up to develop strategies for pupil management

School supported the introduction and use of the system meetings with YLL and other groups to discuss implementation. Support from Admin in implementing exit procedures.

feedback survey re: pupil perceptions

Staff who felt that insufficient support was given provided a range of suggestions including the belief that the administration was 'Too busy/ Unavailability' at times, that there was a 'Lack of communication', or that the structures/processes were 'Ineffective':

Often staff, colleagues, don't know the situation or are too involved with their own problems to provide full support.

Coordinators and welfare staff do their best but lack of time makes it very difficult for them to always follow up.

Sometimes it is difficult for the management to deal with a lot of different issues; they are overwhelmed.

Hardly any feedback is given when referrals are made.

Coordinator followed up incident; pupils exited but no feedback on what followed.

sometimes no knowledge of serious issues being followed up

need for a more effective welfare system, thus knowledge made available to teachers on pupil background and present problems not sound management structures for dealing with repeated offenders

We have not agreed upon 2/3 expectations as requested.

Other teachers discussed a 'Lack of understanding' of the approaches instigated, as well as a 'Lack of consistency' in approaches of coordinators, while others believed there was a 'Lack of ownership' on the teacher's behalf:

more acknowledgement of the difficulties of teaching and the need for exit/time-out supervision of difficult pupils

Admin has no real understanding of this actual concept. They misinterpret this style of discipline as relationship-building when it really is a lot more clinical than that.

depends who is coordinator

Some coordinators are fabulous and are able to present a united front, so positive support with classroom teachers in the face of very difficult behaviour. Others do not inspire confidence.

In some situations it has been fully supportive, but in others, while the intention is there, it has not worked to my satisfaction because it was a coordinator–pupil agreement etc. and not myself–pupil. Consequently, patterns of this behaviour appear all too frequently.

In summarising teachers' comments on the support component of the DMA, it can be seen that most staff acknowledge that support processes are in place and that there is a developing (but not necessarily uniformly successful) culture of support within their schools. Although the teachers' perceptions appear more positive than those normally reported (Rogers, 2002), there is clearly room for improvement. Some of the desired improvement, however, appears to rely on additional resources, mainly in the form of time and staffing. The school-wide nature of DMA is reported as a particular advantage, as is the buddy system and the ongoing focus on professional conversations. Nevertheless, enough concern is expressed to indicate that there are numerous weak spots in the support structures, both collegial and administrative. The need for an ongoing emphasis on maintaining and strengthening the focus is apparent. As one principal said to me when I began to work with his school, 'It will take at least six years to create a genuine, effective culture of support'. Three years to go?

> Most staff acknowledge that support processes are in place and that there is a developing … culture of support within their schools.

10 | Conclusion

It is clear from the analyses presented in this book that in both primary and secondary schools, teacher aggression and, to a lesser extent, punishment are ineffective in fostering positive pupil affect and behaviour. In contrast, Hinting, Discussions, Recognition, and Involvement appear helpful in this regard. Nevertheless, the more difficult pupils frequently experience more of the former, but no more of the latter. It is not surprising that pupils who are subject to, or witness, more teacher aggression, or even escalating punishment in the face of resistance, may react negatively towards the teacher, and be more distrustful of the teacher's perceived intentions, as discussed in Chapter 2.

However, as stated earlier, when a teacher provides recognition and reward for appropriate behaviour (particularly for that of difficult pupils) he or she demonstrates that it is the pupil's behaviour that is the focus of the disciplinary interventions and not a dislike of the child. It is reasonable to expect that such teachers are more likely to be trusted when they do need to deal with misbehaviour.

Similarly, a teacher who talks to misbehaving pupils about his or her concern over the impact their behaviour has on other pupils directly confronts the challenging pupils' hypothesis that they, not the behaviour, are the target of the disciplinary intervention. Therefore, it is to be expected that a more frequent use of discussions would result in a more positive pupil affect.

That being the case, it is problematic to note that teachers dealing with less responsible pupils are not more likely (and in some cases are less likely) to be using productive power such as Reward and Referent power manifested in strategies such as Hinting, Discussing, Recognising and Involving. It is equally problematic to see an increased use of Coercive power in the form of Aggression and Punishment, since they are at best of limited usefulness, and at worst counterproductive in terms of the pupils' attitude to the teacher, their concentration on their work, and their evaluation of the need for teacher intervention.

If teachers are reacting to the level of responsibility displayed by pupils, it is possible that when more pupils misbehave, teachers may become overwhelmed by the level of activity and consequently frustrated. Teachers with insufficient power in the classroom may feel confronted by their own lack of ability to ensure that all pupils are learning and are respectful of rights. According to the levels of aggression reported in Chapter 2, they may even become angry and hostile towards less responsible pupils.

The emotionality in teachers' responses may not only be related to the number of pupils misbehaving but could also be influenced by the perceived severity of the misbehaviour. For example, according to one of the teachers interviewed by Andy Hargreaves (2000, p. 819), commenting on a 5-year-old boy who refused demands to go to the principal, 'You can't help but get angry and agitated when those kinds of things happen.'

Angry or upset teachers may, as argued by William Glasser (1997), not be interested in being reasonable towards unreasonable and disrespectful pupils. Therefore, they may find it unpalatable to recognise difficult pupils when they act appropriately. Similarly, they may find it unpleasant and unproductive to spend time letting such pupils tell their side of events, trying to get them to acknowledge that their behaviour is unfair and needs to change.

Possibly because of teachers' non-productive responses to these more difficult pupils, approximately a third of the pupils in Australian classrooms appear more than sometimes 'distracted' when their teacher deals with misbehaviour. As a result of witnessing, or being the target of, such a disciplinary response, many also see the teacher's behaviour as unjustified and feel more negatively towards the teacher. The proportion of pupils affected is large enough to be of concern. If teachers were more aware of the negative impact their disciplinary behaviour has on pupils' concentration on their schoolwork they might rate their concern about misbehaviour and classroom discipline as higher than moderate.

> First, don't escalate, de-escalate!
> Second, let pupils save face.

There are many reasons to be concerned over teachers' use of aggressive disciplinary techniques, some of which have been covered in earlier chapters. For example, the two most important pieces of advice offered by Margaret Metzger (2002) to teachers trying to ensure that pupils will remain motivated to behave responsibly are: first, don't escalate, de-escalate! second, let pupils save face.

Clearly, both of these processes, which would generate Referent power, are incompatible with an aggressive teacher response to misbehaviour, and may also be at variance with escalating punishment in the face of resistance (especially for the more difficult Category C and D pupils). A second reason to ensure teachers minimise the use of aggressive responses towards pupils is the need to provide an appropriate model for children. The tendency by a large minority of teachers to display a relative unwillingness to use strategies with the more difficult pupils such as Discussion, Recognition and Reward, and Involvement is also problematic. The concern generally relates to the educational purpose of classroom discipline discussed in Chapter 1. First, as shown in Chapter 5, and as argued by a number of experienced educators, these three strategies are among those essential for producing responsible pupils (Metzger, 2002; Roeser *et al.*, 2000; Ryan and Patrick, 2001). As stated by Peggy Pastor (2000, p. 657), when determining which discipline strategies are the most desirable, we need to note that:

> When we separate our approach to discipline from our principles, we influence the ethical tone of the school community. Valuing good character and seeking the development of personal responsibility determine the school's response to discipline problems. Discipline is not primarily a matter of keeping things under control by making choices for students … it is a matter of helping students learn to make good choices and be responsible for those choices.

In discussing the alternatives for discipline, Martin Maehr and Carole Midgeley (1991, p. 412) make a similar point, highlighting the limitations of Coercive power in comparison to Referent power when they state: 'Discipline procedures can reflect sheer force or attempts to develop critical thinking about implications of one's behaviour.' In supporting a recommendation for more inclusion of pupils' voices, Metzger (2002, p. 657) focuses on the relevance of discipline to the development of democratic citizens when she states: 'As we seek to prepare children to be productive citizens of a democracy, teaching them to understand and exercise their choices and voices becomes paramount.'

The final comment on the relevance of the DMA to teachers and pupils relates to an observation by Robert Roeser *et al.* (2000, p. 466), commenting on how to facilitate the likelihood of teachers' increasing their use of Referent power while decreasing their Coercive power, including aggressive responses, even to the most difficult of pupils.

> Creating professional work environments where teachers feel supported by other professionals and school leaders in relation to their own needs for competence, autonomy, and quality relationships is essential to their decision to create these conditions for students.

References

Ainley, J., Batten, M., Collins, C., and Withers, G. (1998). *Schools and the social development of young Australians.* Melbourne: ACER.

Akin-Little, K. A., Eckert, T. L., Lovett, B. J., and Little, S. G. (2004). Extrinsic reinforcement in the classroom: Bribery or best practices. *School Psychology Review, 33,* 344–62.

Anderman, Eric M. (2002). School effects on psychological outcomes during adolescence. *Journal of Educational Psychology, 94*(4), 795–809.

Axelrod, S. (1996). What's wrong with behaviour analysis? *Journal of Behavioural Education, 6,* 247–56.

Balson, M. (1992). *Understanding classroom behaviour* (3rd ed.). Melbourne: ACER.

Bandura, A. (1994). *Self-efficacy in changing societies.* Cambridge University Press.

Barton, P. E., Coley, R. J., and Wenglinsky, H. (1998). *Order in the classroom: Violence, discipline and student achievement.* Princeton, NJ: Policy Information Center. Educational Testing Service.

Beck, J., and Horne, D. (1992). A whole school implementation of the Stop, Think Do! Social skills training program at Minerva Special School. In B. Willis and J. Izard (Eds.), *Student behaviour problems: Directions, perspectives and expectations.* Melbourne: ACER.

Beck, M., and Malley, J. A. (1998). Pedagogy of belonging: Reclaiming children and youth. *Journal of Emotional and Behavioural Problems, 7*(3), 133–37.

Bennett, W. (1988). The place to harvest patriots. *School-Administrator, 55*(5), 38–40.

Bernard, M. (1990). *Taking the stress out of teaching.* Melbourne: Collins Dove.

Berne, E. (1961). *Transactional analysis in psychotherapy: A systematic individual and social psychiatry.* New York: Grove Press.

Berne, E. (1964). *Games people play: The psychology of human relationships.* London: Andre Deutsch.

Borg, I. (1992). Absence from school and mental health. *British Journal of Psychiatry, 161*, 154–66.

Borg, M. G., Riding, R. J., and Falzon, J. M. (1991). Stress in teaching: A study of occupational stress and its determinants, job satisfaction and career commitment among primary schoolteachers. *Educational Psychology, 11*(1), 59–75.

Bowlby, J. (1975). *Separation: Anxiety and anger* vol. 2. Harmondsworth: Penguin.

Bowlby, J. (1981). *Loss, sadness and depression* vol. 3. Harmondsworth: Penguin.

Bowlby, J. (1982). *Attachment* (2nd ed.) vol. 1. London: Harper Collins.

Bruce, K. and Cacioppe, R. (1989). A survey of why teachers resigned from government secondary schools in Western Australia. *Australian Journal of Education, 33*(1), 68–82.

Buisson, G. J., Murdock, J. Y., Reynolds, K. E., and Cronin, M. E. (1995). Effect of tokens on response latency of students with hearing impairments in a resource room. *Education and Treatment of Children, 18*, 408–21.

Canter, L., and Canter, M. (1996). *Assertive discipline: A take charge approach for today's educators* (3rd ed.). USA: Lee Canter and Associates.

Cavalier, A. R., Ferretti, R. P., and Hodges, A. E. (1997). Self-management within a classroom token economy for students with learning disabilities. *Research in Developmental Disabilities, 18*, 167–78.

Chan, D. W. (1998). Stress, coping strategies, and psychological distress among secondary teachers in Hong Kong. *American Educational Research Journal, 35*(1), 145–63.

Commonwealth of Australia (2005). *National framework for values education in Australian schools.* Department of Education, Science and Training, Australian Government, Canberra, accessed 3 Sept. 2007. <http://www.valueseducation.edu.au/verve/_resources/Framework_PDF_version_for_the_web.pdf>.

Crawford, F., and Beaman, R. (2007). Managing classroom behaviour. *Curriculum Leadership, 5* (38), taken from <www.curriculum.edu.au/leader/managing_classroom_behaviour,14728.html>.

Curriculum Corporation (1997). *Discovering Democracy,* Melbourne: Curriculum Corporation.

Deci, E. L., Koestner, R., and Ryan, R. M. (1999a). A meta-analytic review of experiments examining the effects of extrinsic rewards on intrinsic motivation. *Psychological Bulletin, 125*, 627–68.

Deci, E. L., Koestner, R., and Ryan, R. M. (1999b). The undermining effect is a reality after all-extrinsic rewards, task interest, and self-determination. Reply to Eisenberger, Pierce, and Cameron (1999) and Lepper, Henderlong, and Gingras (1999). *Psychological Bulletin, 125*, 692–700.

Deci, E. L., Koestner, R., Ryan, R. M. (2001). Extrinsic rewards and intrinsic motivation in education: Reconsidered once again. *Review of Educational Research, 71*, 1–27.

DeRobbio, R., and Iwanicki, E. (1996). Factor accounting for burnout among secondary school teachers. Paper presented at the annual meeting of the American Educational Research Association, New York.

Dreikurs, R., and Cassel, P. (1972). *Discipline without tears* (rev. ed.). New York: Hawthorn Books.

Edwards, D., and Mullis, F. (2003). Classroom meetings: Encouraging a climate of cooperation. *Professional School Counseling, 7*(1) American School Counselor Assn, US., 20–28.

Ellis, J., Hart, S., and Small-McGinley, J. (1998). The perspectives of difficult students on belonging and inclusion in the classroom. *Reclaiming Children and Youth: Journal of Emotional and Behavioural Problems, 7*(3), 142–46.

Emmer, E. T., and Aussiker A. (1990). School and classroom discipline programs: How well do they work? In Moles, Oliver C. *et al.* (Eds.). *Student discipline strategies: Research and practice.* SUNY series in educational leadership. Albany, NY: State University of New York Press, 129–65.

Fenstermacher, G. D. (2001). On the concept of manner and its visibility in teaching practice. *Journal of Curriculum Studies, 33*(6), 639–53.

Fields, B. (1986) The nature and incidence of classroom behaviour problems and their remediation through preventive management. *Behaviour Change, 3*(1), 53–57.

Fisher, D., Henderson, D., and Fraser, B. (1997). Laboratory environments and student outcomes in senior school biology. *American Biology Teacher, 59*(2), 14–19.

Freiberg, H. J. (1996). From tourists to citizens in the classroom. *Educational Leadership, 54*(1), 32–36.

Freiberg H. J., Stein, T. A., and Huang, S. (1995). Effects of a classroom management intervention on student achievement in inner-city elementary schools. *Educational Research and Evaluation, 1*(1), 36–66.

French, J. R. P., and Raven, B. H. (1959). The bases of social power. In I. D. Cartwright (Ed.), *Studies in Social Power.* Ann Arbor, MI: Institute for Social Research, 150–67.

Friedman, I. A. (1995). Student behaviour patterns contributing to teacher burnout. *Journal of Educational Research, 88*(5), 281–89.

Friedman, I. A. (2006). Classroom management and teacher stress and burnout. In C. M. Evertson and C. S. Weinstein (Eds.), *Handbook of classroom management: Research, practice and contemporary issues*. New Jersey: Lawrence Erlbaum Associates Inc., 925–44.

Fuller, F. F., and Bown, O. H. (1975). Becoming a teacher. In K. Ryan (Ed.), *Teacher education*. The seventy-fourth yearbook of the National Society for the Study of Education, part 2. Chicago University Press.

Gardener, H. (1983). *Frames of mind: The theory in practice*. New York: Basic Books.

Giedd, J. N. (2004). Structural magnetic resonance imaging of the adolescent brain. *Annals of the New York Academy of Sciences, 1021*(1), 77–85.

Glasser, W. (1969). *School without failure*. New York. Harper and Row.

Glasser, W. (1984). *Control theory*. New York: Harper and Row.

Glasser, W. (1986). *Control theory in the classroom*. New York: Perennial Library.

Glasser, W. (1997). A new look at school failure and school success. *Phi Delta Kappan, 78*(8), 597–602.

Goddard, J. T. (2000). Teaching in turbulent times: Teachers' perceptions of the effects of external factors on their professional lives. *Alberta Journal of Educational Research, 46*(4), 293–310.

Gordon, T. (1970). *Parent effectiveness training: The tested new way to raise responsible children*. New York: P. H. Wyden.

Gordon, T. (1974). *T.E.T.: Teacher Effectiveness Training*. New York: D. McKay.

Gottfredson, D. C., Karweit, N. L., and Gottfredson, G. D. (1989). *Reducing disorderly behavior in middle schools*. Baltimore, MD: Center for Research on Elementary and Middle Schools, Johns Hopkins University.

Greaves, D. (1987). Between the tides: Discipline problems in the classroom. In *Special Education for Effective Integration*. Melbourne: R. D. Printworks.

Green, S. B., and Ross, M. E. (1996). A theory-based measure of coping strategies used by teachers: The problems in Teaching Scale. *Teaching and Teacher Education, 12*(30), 315–25.

Handelsman, D. J., and Gupta, L. (1997). Prevalence and risk factors for anabolic-androgenic steroid abuse in Australian high school students. *International Journal of Andrology, 20*(3), 159–64.

Hansen, D. T. (2001). Reflections on the manner in teaching project. *Journal of Curriculum Studies, 33*(6), 729–35.

Hardman, E. L., and Smith, S. W. (2003). Analysis of classroom discipline-related content in elementary education journals. *Behavioural Disorders, 28*, 173–86.

Hargreaves, A. (2000). Mixed emotions: Teachers' perceptions of their interactions with students. *Teaching and Teacher Education, 16*, 811–26.

Hart, P. M., Wearing, A. J., and Conn, M. (1995). Conventional wisdom is a poor predictor of the relationship between discipline policy, student misbehaviour and teacher stress. *British Journal of Educational Psychology, 65*(1), 27–48.

Hastings, N. and Schwieso, J. (Eds.) (1995). *New directions in educational psychology* vol. 2. London: Falmer Press.

Heider, F. (1958). *The psychology of interpersonal relations.* New York: Wiley.

Henderson, D., Fisher, D., and Fraser, B. J. (2000). Interpersonal behaviour, learning environments and student outcomes in senior biology classes. *Journal of Research in Science Teaching, 37*, 26–43.

Houston, P. D. (1998). The centrality of character education. *School Administrator, 55*(5), 6–8.

Hyman, I. A., and Snook, P. A. (2000). Dangerous schools and what you can do about them. *Phi Delta Kappan, 81*(7), 489–501.

Independent Education Union (1996). *Education and Stress: Report on the survey conducted by the Victoria and NSW IEU on workloads and perceptions of occupational stress among union members employed in Catholic schools, and Education Offices and in Independent schools.* Melbourne: IEU.

Ingersoll, R. M. (1996). Teachers' decision-making power and school conflict. *Sociology of Education, 68*(2), 159–76.

Ingersoll, R. M. (2001). Teacher turnover and teacher shortages: An organizational analysis. *American Educational Research Journal, 38*(3), 499–534.

Ingvarson, L. (2005). *Getting professional development right.* ACER Annual Conference Proceedings 2005, Using data to support student learning. Melbourne: ACER.

Isaacson, C., and Radish, K. (2002). *The birth order effect.* Adams Media.

Johnson, B., Oswald, M., and Adey, K. (1993). Discipline in South Australian primary schools, *Educational Studies, 19*(3), 289–305.

Jones, E. E., and Davis, K. E. (1965). From acts to dispositions: The attribution process in person perception. In L. Berkowitz (Ed.), *Advances in Experimental Social Psychology* vol. 2. Orlando, FL: Academic Press.

Jones, S. C., and Stoodley, J. (1999). Community of caring: A character education program designed to integrate values into a school community. *NASSP, 83*(609), 46–51.

Keiper, R., and Busselle, K. (1996). The rural educator and stress. *Rural Educator, 17*(2), 18–21.

Kelley, H. H. (1973). The processes of causal attribution. *American Psychologist, 28*, 107–28.

Kohn, A. (1993). *Punished by rewards: The trouble with gold stars, incentive plans, A's, praise, and other bribes.* Boston, MA: Houghton Mifflin.

Kohn, A. (1996). *Beyond discipline: From compliance to community.* Alexandria, VA: Association for Supervision and Curriculum Development.

Kounin, J. S. (1970). *Discipline and group management in classrooms.* New York: Holt, Rinehart and Winston, Inc.

Lazear, D. (1999). *Eight ways of knowing: Teaching for multiple intelligences: A handbook of techniques for expanding* (3rd ed.). Melbourne: Hawker Brownlow Education.

Leman, K. (1985). *The birth order book: Why you are the way you are.* New York: Dell Publishing Leman.

Lewis, R. (1997a). Discipline in schools. In L. J. Saha (Ed.), *International encyclopedia of the sociology of education.* Oxford: Permagon, 404–11.

Lewis, R. (1997b). *The discipline dilemma* (2nd ed.) Melbourne: ACER.

Lewis, R. (1999a). Preparing students for democratic citizenship: Codes of conduct in Victoria's 'Schools of the Future'. *Educational Research and Evaluation, 5*, 141–61.

Lewis, R. (1999b). Teachers coping with the stress of classroom discipline. *Social Psychology of Education, 3*, 1–17.

Lewis, R. (2001). Classroom discipline and student responsibility: The students' view. *Teaching and Teacher Education, 17*(3), 307–19.

Lewis, R. (2006). Classroom discipline in Australia. In C. M. Evertson and C. S. Weinstein (Eds.), *Handbook of classroom management: Research, practice and contemporary issues.* New Jersey: Lawrence Erlbaum Associates Inc., 1193–214.

Lewis, R., and Burman, E. (2006). Providing for student voice in classroom management. *International Journal of Inclusive Education, 10*(6).

Lewis, R., and Frydenberg, E. (2002). Concomitants of failure to cope: What we should teach adolescents about coping. *British Journal of Educational Psychology, 72*, 419–31.

Lewis, R., and Frydenberg, E. (2004). Adolescents least able to cope: How do they respond to their stresses? *British Journal of Guidance and Counselling, 32*(1), 25–38.

Lewis, R., and Lovegrove. M. N. (1987a). The teacher as a disciplinarian: How do students feel? *Australian Journal of Education, 31*(2), 173–86.

Lewis, R., and Lovegrove, M. N. (1987b). What students think of teachers' classroom control techniques: Results from four studies. In

N. Hastings and J. Schwieso. (Eds.), *New directions in educational psychology* vol. 2. London: Falmer Press, 93–113.

Lewis, R., and Lovegrove, M. (1988). Students' views on how teachers are disciplining classrooms. In R. Slee (Ed.), *Discipline and schools: A curriculum perspective*. Melbourne: Macmillan, 268–83.

Lewis, R., Lovegrove, M. N., and Burman, E. (1991). Teachers' perceptions of ideal classroom disciplinary practices. In M. N. Lovegrove and R. Lewis (Eds.), *Classroom discipline*. Melbourne: Longman Cheshire, 86–113.

Lewis, R., Romi, S., Qui, X., and Katz, Y. J. (2005). Teachers' classroom discipline and student misbehaviour in Australia, China and Israel. *Teaching and Teacher Education, 21,* 729–41.

Lewis, R., Romi, S., Qui, X., and Katz, Y. J. (2007). Students' reactions to teachers' classroom discipline techniques in China, Australia and Israel. *Teaching and Teacher Education.*

Lickona, T. (1996). Teaching respect and responsibility: Reclaiming children and youth. *Journal of Emotional and Behavioural Problems, 5*(3), 143–51.

Liu, X., and Meyer, J. P. (2005). Teachers' perceptions of their jobs: A multi-level analysis of the teacher follow-up survey for 1994–95. *Teachers' College Record, 107*(5), 985–1003.

Luna, B., and Sweeney, J. A. (2004). The emergence of collaborative brain function: fMRI studies of the development of response inhibition. *Annals of the New York Academy of Sciences, 1021*(1), 296–309.

Macciomei, N. R. (1999). Behavioral problems in urban school children. In N. R. Macciomei and D. H. Ruben (Eds.), *Behavior management in the public schools: An urban approach*. Westport, CT: Praeger, 3–18.

Maehr, M. L., and Midgely, C. (1991). Enhancing student motivation: A schoolwide approach. *Educational Psychologist, 26*(3/4), 399–427.

McCormick, J., and Shi, G. (1999). Teachers' attributions of responsibility for their occupational stress in the People's Republic of China and Australia. *British Journal of Educational Psychology, 69*(3), 393–407.

McDonnell, S. (1998). Ethics and freedom. *School Administrator, 55*(5), 18–20.

McInerney, D., and McInerney, V. (2002). *Educational psychology: Constructing learning* (3rd ed.). Sydney: Prentice Hall.

Mellor, S., Kennedy, K., and Greenwood, L. (2001). *Citizenship and democracy: Students' knowledge and beliefs, Australian 14 Year olds and the Civic Education study*. Melbourne: ACER.

Metzger, M. (2002). Learning to discipline. *Phi Delta Kappan, 84*(1), 77–84.

Milgram, S. (1975). *Obedience to authority: An experimental view.* New York: Harper and Row.

Moore, M. (2004), quoted from article in press: Outsiders fit into special programs. *The Age*, Melbourne, 14 June 2004.

Osler, A., and Starkey, H. (2001). Citizenship education and natural identities in France and England: Inclusive or exclusive? *Oxford Review of Education, 27*(2), 287–305.

Oswald, U., Johnson, B., and Whittington, V. (1997). Classroom discipline problems in South Australian Government and Independent Schools. Paper presented at Australian Association of Educational Research Conference. <http://www.aare.edu.au/97pap/oswam463.htm>.

Pastor, P. (2000). School discipline and the character of our schools. *Phi Delta Kappan, 83*(9), 658–61.

Pearl, A., and Knight, A. (1998). *Democratic Schooling: Theory to Guide Educational Practice.* New Jersey: Hampton Press.

Piekarska, A. (2000). School stress, teachers' abusive behaviours and students' coping strategies. *Child Abuse and Neglect, 11*, 1443–49.

Pithers, R. T., and Soden, R. (1998). Scottish and Australian teacher stress and strain: A comparative study. *British Journal of Educational Psychology, 68*, 269–79.

Pring, R. (2000). Education as a moral practice. *Journal of Moral Education, 30*(2), 101–12.

Punch, K. F., and Tuetteman, E. (1996). Reducing teacher stress: The effects of support in the work environment. *Research in Education, 56*, 63–72.

Roeser, R. W., Eccles, J. S., and Sameroff, A. J. (2000). School as a context of early adolescents' academic and social-emotional development: A summary of the research findings. *The Elementary School Teacher, 11*(5), 443–71.

Rogers, W. (1992). *Supporting teachers in the workplace.* Milton, Qld: Jacaranda Press.

Rogers, W. (2002). *I get by with a little help ... Colleague support in schools.* Melbourne: ACER.

Romi, S., Lewis, R. and Katz, Y. J. (2007). Student responsibility and classroom discipline in Australia, China and Israel. Unpublished manuscript.

Rothstein, R. (2000). Towards a composite index of school performance. *The Elementary School Teacher, 100*(5), 409–41.

Rowe, K. S., and Rowe, K.J. (2006). Careful, he may not hear you: Or, more accurately, may not process auditory information. *Teacher: The National Education Magazine*, May, 60–63.

Ryan, K., and Patrick, H. (2001). The classroom social environment and changes in adolescents' motivation and engagement in the middle school. *American Educational Research Journal, 38*(2), 437–60.

Sava, F. A. (2002). Causes and effects of teacher conflict-inducing attitudes towards pupils: A path analysis model. *Teaching and Teacher Education, 18*, 1007–21.

Schneider, E. (1996). Giving students a voice in the classroom. *Educational Leadership, 54*(1), 22–26.

Slee, R. (Ed.) (1988). *Discipline and schools: A curriculum perspective.* Melbourne: Macmillan.

Spear, L. P. (2000). The adolescent brain and age-related behavioural manifestations. *Neuroscience and Biobehavioural Reviews, 24*(2000), 417–63.

Strauch, B. (2003). *Why are they so weird? What's really going on in a teenager's brain.* London: Bloomsbury.

Swiezy, N. B., Matson, J. L., and Box, P. (1992). The good behaviour game: A token reinforcement system for preschoolers. *Child and Family Behaviour Therapy, 14*, 21–32.

Swinson, J., and Cording, M. (2002). Assertive discipline in a school for pupils with emotional and behavioural difficulties. *British Journal of Special Education, 29*(2), 72–75.

Swinson, J., and Melling, R. (1995). Assertive discipline: Four wheels on this wagon: A reply to Robinson and Maines. *Educational Psychology in Practice, 11*(3), 3–8.

Tauber, R. (2007). *Classroom management: Sound theory and effective practice.* Westport, CT: Greenwood Publishers.

Thomas, R. M. (2000). *Comparing theories of child development* (5th ed.). Belmont, CA: Wadsworth/Thomson Learning.

Veenman, S., Voeten, M., and Lem, P. (1987). Classroom time and achievement in mixed age classes. *Educational Studies, 13*(1), 75–89.

Vitto, J. M. (2003). *Relationship-driven classroom management strategies that promote student motivation.* Thousand Oaks, CA: Corwin Press, Inc., Sage Publications.

Wade, R. K. (1997). Lifting a school's spirit. *Educational Leadership, 54*(8), 34–36.

Weiner, B. (1985). An attributional theory of achievement motivation and emotion. *Psychological Review, 92*, 548–73.

Weiner, B. (1994). Integrating social and personal theories of achievement striving. *Review of Educational Research, 64*, 557–73.

White, R., and Gunstone, R. (1992). *Probing understanding*. London, New York: Falmer.

Whiteman, J. L., Young, J. C., and Fisher, L. (1985). Teacher burnout and the perception of student behaviour. *Education, 105*, 299–305.

Wolfgang, C. H. (1995). *Solving discipline problems: Strategies for classroom teachers* (3rd ed). Massachusetts: Allyn and Bacon.

Zbar, V., Brown, D., Bereznicki, B., and Hooper, C. (2003). *Values education study: Final report*. Zbar Consulting; Curriculum Corporation; University of Melbourne.

Index